# 'TWIXT
# WO...
# CARR &
# COAST

## East Yorkshire
## MOTOR SERVICES LTD

### and its associates

## Keith A. Jenkinson

**An Autobus Review Publication**

*First published February 1992*

ISBN 0 907834 21 3

*Front cover upper : Showing the need for its specially-contoured roof, traditional liveried 1957 Roe-bodied AEC Regent V 652 passes beneath the Gothic arch of Beverley Bar on a Limited Stop journey to Hull.*

*Front cover lower : Amongst the more recent additions to East Yorkshire's fleet is 550, an NCME-bodied Leyland Olympian purchased new in 1990. It is seen here outside Hull's Ferensway Coach Station whilst operating the service to Hessle.   (J.Whiteing)*

*Below : The name East Yorkshire Motor Services almost always conjures up memories of double deck buses with specially-shaped roofs necessary to allow them to pass beneath the Gothic arch of Beverley Bar before this was circumnavigated by the opening of a new road. Illustrating this are a pair of AEC Regent Vs alongside a low-height AEC Renown the top deck of which was tapered inward for this same purpose.   (D.J.Stanier)*

*Design & typeset by Autobus Studios.*

*Printed by Bakes & Lord Ltd., Beacon Road, Bradford BD6 3NB.*

*Autobus Review Publications Ltd., 42 Coniston Avenue, Queensbury, Bradford BD13 2JD.*

# FOREWORD

Much has happened since East Yorkshire Motor Services was privatised in February 1987, and exactly five years on it is very pleasing to know that the company's history is being brought up to date.

Now part of the EYMS Group Limited which also has a number of other subsidiaries, East Yorkshire is probably as strong and healthy now as it has ever been. It is almost a family concern once again, with just two shareholder directors closely involved in the day to day running of the business - for business it surely now is. We have been very happy to take such a good company forward, firstly into deregulation, and now into the '90's and hopefully on into the 21st century.

East Yorkshire has, we believe, a very good name amongst bus enthusiasts and in the public transport world generally, and we welcome this new edition of the East Yorkshire history, which both updates and in some minor cases corrects the earlier edition, but more importantly chronicles the many changes during the last ten years, which have probably been some of the most eventful in the company's history.

P.J.S.Shipp                                        B.G.Burley

February 1992

*P.J.S.Shipp*

*B.G.Burley*

# INTRODUCTION

With its foundations laid in the Hull area in 1919, East Yorkshire Motor Services has now grown to serve a wide area around North Humberside and North Yorkshire and in more recent years has expanded its field of operation as a result of the merging of United's Scarborough and Pickering activities and the acquisition of several smaller companies.

Research relating to the years before 1945 was particularly difficult due to many of the company's records being destroyed in the enemy air attacks on Hull during world war II and it was necessary to make contact with a great number of the company's former employees and the families of operators taken over in the 'twenties and 'thirties.

I claim no credit for the research relating to the period up to 1980, this being painstakingly undertaken by Ian C. Gibbs of Green Hammerton, York to whom I record my sincere thanks. Had it not been for his valiant efforts over a period of ten years, so much would have been left unrecorded and it would have been impossible to produce such a concise history of bus operation in what was once the East Riding of Yorkshire.

As will be seen from the following pages, history has begun to repeat itself with East Yorkshire in recent years swallowing up several of their competitors just as they did in the 'twenties and 'thirties. Despite looking to the future and endeavouring to provide their passengers with the highest standards in service and vehicle types, East Yorkshire have never forgotten their past and have pleasingly maintained a

small fleet of older vehicles which have been restored for special occasional use as a reminder of their earlier history.

Whilst it is impossible to individually thank all those who have assisted with the production of this book, as well as special mention being given to Ian C. Gibbs, my thanks must also be extended to Peter Shipp, Chairman and Joint Managing Director of the EYMS Group for all his help and encouragement and for checking the following text for accuracy. I am also grateful to the EYMS Group for making available their excellent photographic collection from which many of the illustrations in this book have been drawn, and to the numerous other photographers without whose work this publication would have been incomplete. Each picture has been credited individually where the photographer is known, but in a number of cases this has been impossible and therefore a big 'thank you' is also necessary to all those anonymous photographers whose work has enabled several pictorial gaps to be filled.

Finally, I hope that those who read this history gain as much pleasure as I gained in its compilation.

Keith A. Jenkinson,
Queensbury,
Bradford

February 1992

# THE FORMATIVE YEARS

From small acorns grow large oaks, an adage particularly true of the East Yorkshire Motor Services group who have grown from small beginnings soon after World War I into an important company whose buses and coaches are now a familiar sight north of the river Humber in East Yorkshire and in parts of North Yorkshire.

Although it was not until 5 October 1926 that East Yorkshire Motor Services Ltd. came into being, the company's foundations had been laid several years earlier when, in December 1919, Ernest John Lee purchased a 14-seat Ford model T bus and began to operate this between Elloughton and Hull via Brough, Ferriby, Welton and Hessle. Formerly a coachman for Dr.Mountain of Brough, Ernest Lee was left £100 in the will of his former employer and it was with this and £100 savings (earned by refurbishing and selling lorries) that he bought his first bus. The success of his new venture was such that within a short space of time a second vehicle was purchased, this being an Atlas fitted with charabanc bodywork which was employed mainly on private hire work, although when passenger demands were heavy, it too was occasionally used on the Hull service. During 1921 Lee's service was extended from Elloughton to South Cave and to accommodate the growing number of passengers, a third vehicle was added to the fleet in April 1922 in the form of a Leyland C5 with 28-seat charabanc body.

Early in 1922, a Mr.Scaife of Elloughton who had an interest in the affairs of a Mr.R.Beaulah and who lived near Lee's garage at Elloughton offered Ernest Lee financial assistance to enable him to further expand his successful business. A condition of this offer was that Mr.Beaulah was to be taken into partnership and to this, Ernest Lee readily agreed and as a result, the name of the business was changed to Lee & Beaulah. The livery used was the dark blue and primrose originally adopted by Lee and the only outward sign of change was the new fleet name carried by the vehicles concerned.

Further expansion took place in May 1922 when Lee & Beaulah's service was extended onward from South Cave to North Cave and in August of that year, two more buses were added to the fleet with a third joining them in September. These comprised a Leyland G5 with Barnaby 32-seat rear entrance bus body, a Vulcan VSD 32-seat charabanc and a Barnaby-bodied front entrance 26-seat Leyland G7, all of which were purchased new. The fares charged at this time were Elloughton to Hull 1/9d return, Brough to Hull 1/9d return, North Ferriby to Hull 1/4d return and Anlaby to Hull 7d return. Single fares were half the return fare plus 1d. Later in 1922 yet another extension was added to Lee & Beaulah's lucrative route, this being from North Cave to Gilberdyke via Newport and in addition, a run to Howden was introduced, this using a small vehicle which was outstationed at Gilberdyke. Expansion continued throughout 1923/4 during which time a further five vehicles were added to the fleet with eight more arriving in 1925.

1924 proved to be a year of particular development however, with Mr.D.Massey joining Lee & Beaulah as a partner and co-director and the business of W.H.'Pop' Rea being taken over. Rea, a retired sea captain, had purchased a motor garage in Withernsea from a Mr.Simpkins and lived in a house adjoining his business premises. After acquiring a taxi and employing Mr.Simpkin's son, Arthur, as a driver, 'Pop' Rea turned his attention to bus operation and made an offer to J.Symonds for the purchase of his route and vehicles.

Joseph James Symonds, who lived at 'The Laurels', Roos, had started a bus service from Withernsea to Hull on 12 July 1922, this running in direct competition to Burns of Withernsea, an already established operator. Symonds, whose service terminated at Smeaton Street in Hull, operated seven journeys per day using a pair of model-T Ford charabancs. For much of the route, the road surface comprised crushed rubble and the uneven nature of this quickly began to cause a great deal of damage to the Fords, which were not the most sturdy of vehicles. Additionally, the hill at Rimswell often proved too much for these little vehicles and passengers were frequently called upon to 'get out and push' in order to reach the summit. As passenger demand grew, Symonds decided to purchase a larger - and sturdier - vehicle and in May 1923 took delivery of a secondhand Tilling Stevens petrol-electric double decker which, like the Fords, was painted in Symonds' standard livery of yellow and brown. In order to 'crew' this bus (for the Fords had been one-person-operated), Symonds at first employed his house maid as a conductress until a permanent person was appointed to this position. Although this double decker was at first hailed as a great success, it was not long before it began to prove extremely troublesome and in 1924 the Hull Watch Committee refused ro relicense it until it was 'rendered safe by the completion of essential repairs'. In addition, the route upon which it was employed was far from

*Lee & Beaulah started their Brough - Hull service in 1923 using a 14-seat Model-T Ford, BT3966. It is pictured here on its first journey with Mr.E.J.Lee acting as driver/ conductor.*
*(Percival Aircraft Ltd/EYMS)*

*Lee & Beaulah purchased this 40hp Lancia rear entrance single decker in November 1924. Seen here in an all-white livery, it was sold shortly before the formation of East Yorkshire Motor Services. (EYMS)*

*Pictured at Brough Aerodrome, Lee & Beaulah's 23-seat Leyland charabanc BT6134 was purchased new in June 1923. According to the board mounted below its windscreens it was used on the Brough & South Cave service. Passing to East Yorkshire upon its formation, it was eventually withdrawn in 1929. (EYMS)*

ideal for double deck vehicles, the area around the Lelley Valley having trees on both sides of the carriageway which, when in bloom in the summer months caused some distress to unwary passengers travelling on the open top deck. It was a combination of these and other problems which finally persuaded Symonds to sell out to Rea in June 1924.

Returning to Rea, as can be seen from the above, his entry into the bus business was made in June 1924 and although Symonds' three vehicles were all acquired, the Tilling Stevens double decker was only used for about four weeks before it was parked out of use in the yard of the Pier Hotel, Withernsea to await its fate. Its replacement was another Ford T which made its debut in July 1924. This was painted in a red livery and soon afterwards, the two ex.Symond' Fords were also transformed into this new colour schem Due to their poor condition however, it was not long befo replacements were sought, these arriving in the form of Vulcan and a Fiat. No sooner had these taken up their dut than Rea received an offer from Lee & Beaulah for business (the latter had some months earlier planne service to Withernsea and felt that the acquisition c existing operation would be preferable to entering competition, if this was possible). After considering offer, 'Pop' Rea decided to accept, subject to secur permanent employment being offered to himself and F by Lee & Beaulah. Agreement was reached and the d concluded towards the end of July 1924 with Mr.Re

up the position of Inspector with the additional responsibility of organising service operations and the collecting and auditing of the company's parcels agencies.

Meanwhile. Lee & Beaulah began to consolidate their interests and in 1925 purchased the Hull - Withernsea licence of D.W.Burn, Withernsea. During the following tear five more buses were purchased, all of which were of Leyland manufacture. One was an LB5 model with open-top 'ouble deck bodywork which had originally been intended for ' ondon General Omnibus Co. whilst the remaining four ·vlan' '·died PLSC1 Lion saloons with seating for 31
   ` the last of these had been delivered
      aaulah applied to the Hull Watch
      ꞓ their licences to a new company, East
      vices Ltd. which came into being on 5
      ;h more later.

      ituent of East Yorkshire Motor Services
      ꞔration was Hull & District Motor Services
      ;et up in September 1924 by H.A.Hervey
      ꞔd the business of John Wilson of Anlaby.
      actory owner who had moved to Southella
      ꞔlly started in business in Shipley, Yorkshire
      ꞔ canisters for such firms as Sanderson's
      ꞔkitts. His move to Hull was to enable him to
      s main customer, and after successfully
      ꞔduction in his new surrounds, he sold his 'new'
      ꞔkitts in 1912. With the money gained from this
      ꞔased a number of houses in Hornsea and after
      ꞔse, he turned the property into a hotel which he
      ꞔ much publicity in 1913. This venture was to be

*Acquired by East Yorkshire upon its formation in 1926 was Lee & Beaulah's 28-seat all-Leyland G7-type bus BT5599 which dated from September 1922. Seen here at Brough Aerodrome, the destination board across its windscreen indicate that it was used on the South Cave service. (EYMS)*

short-lived however, for a year later the hotel was commandeered by the War Ministry and as a result, he was turned - albeit temporarily - into a gentleman of leisure.

One day early in 1915, he was waiting for a bus to Hull (for he did not drive himself) and after finding that he had just missed one operated by Binningtons (whose history appears later in this story), John Wilson came to the conclusion that the public deserved a better service than that already being provided, and that he was just the man to give them one. Without a great deal of further thought, he despatched himself to London and thence to Maidstone where the Tilling Stevens factory was situated, and after examining their products, placed an order for bus bodies and chassis of this make. It would seem however that the company could not deliver these as speedily as he wanted and so, without further ado, he travelled to Liverpool where he bought two Garner chassis. These were transported to Hull travelling one on top of the other and soon after their arrival, one

single deck and two double deck bodies arrived from Tilling Stevens. The single deck and one of the double deck bodies were quickly fitted to the Garner chassis and in July 1915 Wilson began to operate a regular service from Kirkella to Hull. The timetable was arranged 'opposite' to Binnington's and the fact that Willerby was at that time a 'railway village' where almost all the workers would have rail passes did not influence Wilson who included Willerby on his route. The fleet name 'Anlaby Motor Bus Co. Ltd.' was adopted from the start of his operations and although there does not appear to have been a standard livery, the majority of the fleet owned in subsequent years were painted dark red. During the early months of Wilson's operations however, the fleet name 'Wagstaff' was applied to some of his buses, although this was soon erased, and the appearance of this has never been clarified unless this was perhaps the name of a former owner of these particular vehicles.

Soon after the service commenced, a Tilling Stevens petrol

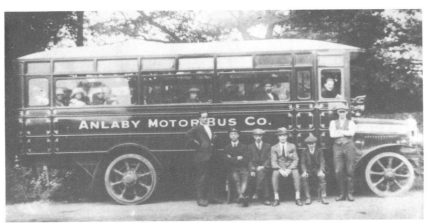

electric chassis was delivered and this was fitted with the spare Tilling double deck body, thus increasing the fleet to three buses. This was given the registration number of the Garner single decker which although no longer used in service, was retained as a spare vehicle.

An unusual arrangement instituted by Wilson related to the takings from the Kirkella - Hull service. As the garage at Kirkella was very close to the village school, the headmaster, a Mr.Ross, collected the money from each run from Wilson's staff and banked this on the company's behalf.

Due to some complication which is not known, the Hull Watch Committee suspended Wilson's licence on 5 January 1916, but in March of that same year reinstated it after additional staff had been obtained. Following this, Wilson turned his thoughts to extending his service from Kirkella through to Elloughton, but this was not proceded with. Sadly, before any further development could take place, on 1 March 1917 at the age of 68, John Wilson died of a heart attack sustained whilst running to catch one of his own buses. Fortunately, Wilson had the services of extremely good accountants, Messrs. Buckley, Hall & Devlin & Co. and immediately after his untimely demise, Wilson's family asked them to continue the business on their behalf. Prior to this, the accountants had employed a Mr.Rushton as manager with a brief to run Wilson's services for him and this arrangement they agreed to continue. Mr.Jackson of Anlaby Park Motors was appointed to succeed Mr.Rushton and in July 1917 Messrs. Buckley, Hall & Devlin & Co. applied to take over Wilson's licences and continue to operate them under the Anlaby Motor Bus Co. name. Few changes were made during the years which followed and it was not until 1920 that any further vehicles were purchased. The first of these was a Tilling Stevens TS3 model with 32-seat charabanc bodywork and this was followed two years later by two more Tilling Stevens petrol-electrics, one a TS3X with 32-seat charabanc body, the other a double decker with wooden, open-top bodywork.

*Posed for the camera in its home village in 1926 is Lawson of Walkington's Ford model-T bus BT8710 which was purchased new in July 1925 and carries its fleet name 'The People's Service' in its side windows.*

*Below : Noel Thompson's fleet in October 1926 when acquired by East Yorkshire comprised from left to right - Dennis BT9808, Leyland A13s BT8981 & BT8777, Vulcan BT7853, Ford T BT4718, Atlas AT6517 and Ford T BT8549.*

In January 1922, the firm had experienced competition on part of its route from a new operator, Captain J. Clark who, on returning from the sea, had decided to invest some of his savings in a new bus company which he set up under the title of 'Anlaby Park Motors'. Starting his operations with a Baico-extended Ford model T single decker and a secondhand Tilling Stevens TTA1 open-top double decker, he began to run between Anlaby Park and Hull, directly competing with Binningtons and the Anlaby Motor Bus Co. Towards the end of the year he had a new garage built at Anlaby Common and soon afterwards added a third bus to his fleet, this being a 30-seat Thornycroft single decker. Within a couple of months, a 14-seat Fiat had also been purchased and Clark's success prompted Buckley, Hall & Devlin to approach him with a view to merging their two

companies. Captain Clark found this proposition attractive, especially as he was promised control of the new combined business and the merger was successfully completed early in 1923. As a result, Anlaby Motor Bus Co's garage at Kirkella was sold to a Mr.Hodgson who was in business as a local haulier, and the whole of the fleet was thereafter concentrated at Clark's garage at Anlaby Common. Further Tilling Stevens petrol-electric buses were added to the fleet and the number of licences was increased to eleven.

Next on the scene came H.A.Harvey, a man who was to become prominent in the Hull area during the next few years.Harvey, who originated from Weare, Hereford, in addition to already operating a bus service in Bishop Auckland, Co. Durham, was well established in the field of

*Acquired from Hull & District Motors in 1926, Tilling Stevens TS3X double decker BT4178 had obviously been used at the Derby on Epsom Downs according to the poster on its side panels.*

*New to Lee & Beaulah in 1922, Vulcan VSD BT5265 was sold to Dixon of Preston when only one year old. It did not serve very long with its new owner however and had left his fleet by 1926 when he sold out to Noel Thompson of Sutton.*

*None of these three buses of Laidlaw, Heddon - Vulcan BT5934, Ford-Baico BT4898 and Ford T BT6514 - survived long enough to pass to East Yorkshire along with his business in October 1926.*

*Springville Leyland S4 BT6335 was delivered new in 1923 fitted with single deck bodywork. In passed to East Yorkshire in 1927 soon after receiving its double deck body which had been removed from a Straker Squire. Its original single deck body was, after a period in store, fitted to East Yorkshire's ex.Lee & Beaulah Leyland C7 BT8435.    (Lucas Ltd.)*

*New in 1924, this Leyland G6 single decker - BT7097 fitted with 'Edinburgh'-style bodywork began life with Springville and joined the East Yorkshire fleet in 1927 along with the Hull Road Motor & Electrical Engineering Co.Ltd. (Springville) business.*

bus hire, supplying buses to independent operators on a week by week hire basis. After offering vehicles to independents in the Hull area, he eventually bought a house at Anlaby Park and decided to make an entry as an operator. Trading as 'White Star', he licensed five vehicles with Hull Watch Committee on 19 September 1924 and a further two in October of that same year. Within a month, Harvey applied for a licence to operate a service from Hull to Cottingham via Newbald, Little Weighton and Skidby but was refused, the reason being that in the opinion of the Watch Committee this area was already adequately served. Undeterred, Harvey successfully applied for a service from Driffield to Bridlington and began operations in December 1924. Almost as soon as he became established, he approached Buckley, Hall & Devlin who, together with Clark were still running Anlaby Motor Bus Co. with a view to merging with them. After much discussion, agreement was reached by all the parties concerned and at the end of 1924, Hull & District Motor Services, with Harvey at the helm, was registered to completely absorb White Star and Anlaby Motor Bus Co.

Throughout this period, Harvey - a man of many parts - had been acting as a 'scout' for British Electric Traction and Tillings, searching for businesses which were ripe for picking and advising them of the operators worthy of purchase. As part of his role, he spent numerous long hours persuading operators to sell to the British Automobile Traction Co., and it is assumed that he must have been well rewarded for his efforts.

Not favouring Fords, he quickly sought to establish 'heavier' buses in the Hull & District fleet and during 1925 purchased no fewer than 4 Dennis single deckers and two Tilling Stevens TS6s. Being a man of vision, he saw that a route from Hull to Bridlington would be an asset to the company and as a result, Hull & District applied for a licence from Hull to Driffield to link up with their existing Driffield - Bridlington service. This was granted at the beginning of

August 1925 with a restriction that no passengers could be picked up between Hull and Beverley. Six journeys were operated in each direction each day and the travelling time from Baker Street, Hull to Bridlington was 2 hours. The fare from terminus to terminus was 2/6d single, 4/- return. The growth of Hull & District was so rapid that, during one particular period when they were awaiting delivery of new buses, they had to hire vehicles from other operators in order to maintain their services. One such operator was Sharpes of Hedon whose vehicles were hired for several weeks.

*Seen before passing to East Yorkshire in 1927, Fussey of Cottingham's open-top 4-ton Dennis WF88 is seen here soon after its entry into service in 1926.*

Throughout this period, Harvey was trying to open up further routes in direct competition to other established operators in the hopes of persuading them into the B.A.T. fold and a great deal of pressure was put on some who were reluctant to sell out. Basically, his efforts and tactics succeeded, and in the spring of 1926 he had sufficient firms lined up to enable the Watch Committee to start checking conditions of licences etc. in readiness for the formation of East Yorkshire Motor Services Ltd. Obviously preparing the Hull & District for sale, Harvey bought a further nine buses during the period March to July 1926, these comprised 8 Dennis' (of which one was a double decker) and a Chevrolet.

# EAST YORKSHIRE IS FORMED

East Yorkshire Motor Services Ltd. was registered on 5 October 1926 by the British Automobile Traction Co. Ltd. to take over Lee & Beaulah Ltd. and Hull & District Motor Services Ltd. To ensure that continuity was maintained, E.J.Lee and D.W.Massey (of Lee & Beaulah) and H.A.Harvey (of Hull & District) were appointed to the East Yorkshire board of directors with D.W.Massey becoming the first chairman. Additionally, Messrs. Buckley, Hall & Devlin & Co. were appointed accountants of the new company and W.B.Hall became secretary. The share capital issued was £24,500 in £1 shares of which Thomas Tilling purchased 12,250; B.A.T. took 4,500; J.S.Wills and E Garcke took 1,000 each and the remainder were acquired by the directors, each of whom had to hold 250 shares to qualify their position. In addition to Lee, Massey and Harvey, the other directors at the formation of the new company were R.Tilling (of Thomas Tilling), S.Powell (of Wilson-Powell), W.S.Wreathall (a local farmer) and W.B.Watson.

Starting with a fleet of some 34 buses acquired from Lee & Beaulah and Hull & District and a nucleus of services around the Hull area, the new company adopted Lee & Beaulah's colours of dark blue & primrose. Two depots were maintained - one ex.Lee & Beaulah at Elloughton cross roads, the other being the former Hull & District premises at Anlaby Common, whilst at Withernsea the company owned a bus station at Bannister Street, this having been acquired with the Lee & Beaulah contribution.

In the months preceding the formation of East Yorkshire Motor Services, Harvey had successfully persuaded Laidlaw of Hedon; Lawson of Walkington; D.W.Burn of Withernsea and Thompson of Sutton to sell out to the new company once

it was up and running, and during the latter months of 1926 he lost no time in ensuring that they did so. All four operators were taken over in October 1926.

Robert Calder Laidlaw had started in the bus business in May 1923 with a Ford Baico T-type and a Vulcan, both of which were employed on his only route which ran from Hedon to Hull. In September 1923 another Ford model-T was purchased and in July of the following year the original Ford Baico T was replaced by a new Vulcan TY single decker. The fleet never exceeded three buses and no further routes were opened.

Conversely, David William Burn was a man of ambition. Born in Newcastle upon Tyne in 1872 he first worked at Parson's Turbines in his home town and later moved to Armstrong Whitworth where he was employed as a fitter. Wishing to gain a wider experience of life, he then took the job of chauffeur to a steel financier who travelled extensively in Europe and whilst in his employment, Burns gained an extensive knowledge of driving and foresaw how the motor vehicle was destined to become a popular mode of transport. On returning to England and moving to Hull, he started a cycle building and repair workshop in West Parade around 1921 and during the following year decided to set up in business as a bus operator. His first vehicle was a model-T Ford which was fitted with dual purpose (goods/passenger) 14-seat bodywork, this being licensed on 28 February 1922. Painted in a grey livery, it was not surprising that his route from Hull to Withernsea was locally referred to as the 'Grey Bus Service', although Burn had officially registered his business as 'Burn's Withernsea Bus Service'. A second bus was purchased in June 1922, this being an Atlas fitted with a 14-seat body built locally by Chapman Bros. and at this same time the frequency of the route was increased to give a more

*East Yorkshire's traffic office at Leyton Chambers, Paragon Street, Hull in 1929.   (EYMS)*

*New to Fussey of Cottingham in 1926, 4-ton Dennis BT9820 passed to East Yorkshire with the Fussey business in July 1927 and is seen here in its new owner's livery operating the Hull - Cottingham service in 1931.*

regular service. A month later, Burn purchased the business and premises of S & F. Needler who operated a service in the Withernsea area. As well as a garage in Queen Street, Withernsea being included in the deal, so too was a house, although it is not known if this was retained or was re-sold.

Now concentrating his operations at his new Queen Street garage, Burn continued to expand by opening a second route from Withernsea to Hull, this being less direct and serving several villages enroute. In April 1925 a secondhand Ford T 14-seat charabanc was purchased from J.Cousins of Hull, this arriving in the red livery of its former owner and in September a new 26-seat Leyland A13 single decker was received. This was followed in March 1926 by another vehicle of this type and together they replaced the Atlas and the secondhand Ford T. Before the year ended, yet another new Leyland joined the fleet, this coming in July in the form of a C9 with 26-seat bodywork.

Although Burn sold his three Leylands and two services to East Yorkshire in October 1926 for the sum of £7,100 and leased his Queen Street garage to the company, his association with passenger vehicle operation was by no means over. After moving to new premises in St.Georges Road, Hull, he built a garage at 32, Albert Avenue and started a new private hire business under the name of 'Grey De-Luxe'. Surprisingly he re-entered stage carriage operation again in 1927 when he was granted a licence to operate two services, one from Waterworks Street to Hessle Road, the other from Waterworks Street to the corner of North Road, from 5.30pm on Christmas Day until 2.00am on Boxing Day. These are believed to be amongst the shortest period services ever licensed, operating for just 8 hours 30 minutes each year with two buses, and were repeated in 1928, 1929 and 1930. After this date, Burn concentrated solely on coaching activities and indeed continued to do so until 1980 when control pased to E.G.Russell and his uncle, Mr.Tyler who had for many years been Burn's partners. Grey De-Luxe was finally acquired by the Anlaby-based independent Alpha Coach Company in the 'eighties who, some years later, still retained one of the acquired coaches in Grey De-Luxe colours.

Alan Lawson of Walkington, the son of a wheelwright, was born on 6 September 1901 and began his driving career at the early age of 16. Shortly before his 21st birthday he purchased a secondhand Crossley bus with 14-seat Barnaby

body and commenced operations between Walkington and Beverley where he picked up passengers for Middleton on the Wolds. In addition to this, his first service was supplemented by runs to Driffield from Middleton on Show Days and when any special events were taking place, and private hire work was also undertaken.

At this time, W.Allen of Middleton was also operating a service to Driffield with three buses - a 14-seat Ford TT, a 20-seat Fiat and a 14-seat Minerva charabanc - and it came as something of a surprise to Alan Lawson when he was asked if he wished to purchase Allen's vehicles and route. A figure was agreed and Lawson took over at the start of 1925. Earlier, in August 1924 Lawson had acquired the licence of W.Drake of Beverley who had run a Crossley bus in opposition to W.Allen. Lawson did not however purchase the Crossley which was instead sold to Newingtons. The Driffield service was operated on Thursdays and Saturdays each week which left the opportunity to build up the private hire activites which became an extremely lucrative side of the business. A standard livery of yellow & red was adopted and whilst the name 'Alan Lawson' was carried across the front of each vehicle, the sides were lettered 'The People's Bus Service'. Finding the Ford TT a somewhat unreliable vehicle, a new Ford chassis was purchased in July 1925 and fitted with the body removed from the TT. In order to reduce dead mileage, two buses were kept at Walkington, one at Lockington and one at Middleton, the Walkington premises also selling BP and Shell petrol to the public.

1926 saw Lawson diversify from his normal operations when he accepted a contract from the Ministry of Agriculture to carry foodstuffs from Hull St.Georges Docks to Scarborough and Doncaster wholesalers. This contract proved so profitable that Lawson cut his bus operations to one vehicle which maintained the Beverley - Middleton route, the other three (the Crossley having been sold by now) being

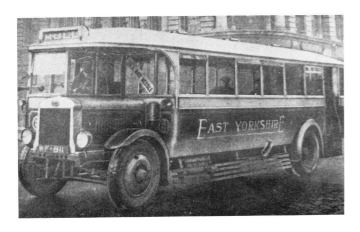

Carrying a paper sticker in its front bulkhead window to inform passengers that it was operating between Hull and Hessle, 1927 Leyland Lion PLSC3 811 (WF811) is seen here after being fitted with a new London Lorries body following the destruction of its original Leyland body when only two months old.

The first new double deckers to be purchased by East Yorkshire arrived in 1929 and were all-Leyland TD1s with open staircase lowbridge bodywork. One of these, 132 is seen here enroute to Hessle in 1931.    (EYMS)

employed each day on the Ministry work. Thus, when Lawson sold out to East Yorkshire on 8 October 1926, he retained all his four vehicles and received but £200 for his solitary service.

The fourth operator to sell to East Yorkshire in October 1926 was Noel Thompson of Sutton in Holderness who had started a service from Sutton to Hull via Stoneferry in July 1921. This at first ran only as far as Sculcoates but was soon extended to Bond Street in the city centre. His first bus was a 20-seat Baico Ford T which had canvas sides and a detachable top and was painted in a grey livery. A second vehicle was purchased in December 1921, this being a 20-seat Overland charabanc, but prior to its arrival, a T-type Ford was hired in order to operate a service from Sutton to the fairground for a week during Hull's famous fair. In June 1922 the original Ford was replaced by a new 14-seat Atlas painted in a red & brown livery which immediately took up its duties on Thompson's solitary route. At this same time, Thompson made an application to the Watch Committee for a licence to operate a service into Hull from Aldborough and after at first deferring their decision, this was eventually granted. Although it is not known for certain, it is believed that whilst awaiting the Watch Committee's decision, Thompson had a change of heart and in the event, never commenced operation of this service.

At the request of the residents of Wawne early in 1923, he started a service from this village to Hull via Sutton, operating it three days per week and in the following year two more vehicles were purchased to meet his extra demands. One was an Atlas lorry which he acquired from Sissons Bros. (Paints) of Hull and fitted with a 14-seat bus body, the other a 14-seat Cubitt which he bought new. By

now he had established a second route from Sutton to Hull, this running via Sutton Ings, and as traffic increased, so he found need for additional and larger vehicles. Consequently, in 1925 he purchased a new 14-seat Ford model T (which replaced one of his older vehicles) and a pair of 26-seat Leyland A13s. Watching all these developments was H.A.Harvey who, seeing the expansion in the Sutton area, applied himself for licences to operate between Hull and Sutton. After a protracted hearing, this was refused by the Watch Committee who informed Harvey that he would not be granted permission to run between these two points by any route. This led Harvey to approach Thompson with an offer to purchase his business, but Thompson, being quite satisfied with his business, declined and immediately approached Cyril Dixon of Preston with a view to an amalgamation. Dixon eventually agreed and by May 1926 had added his Hull - Preston service to those operated by Thompson. Dixon's two Vulcan 26-seat buses were also involved in this agreement and to supplement the fleet, a new 29-seat rear-entrance 50cwt Dennis was purchased in July 1926. Feeling now that they were in a strong position to command a high price, they sold to East Yorkshire in October by which time the licences were all held by Thompson.

Thus, within two months of its formation, East Yorkshire had already acquired four of its competitors and had begun to establish itself as the major operator in the Hull area.

Hall Lewis coach-bodied Leyland TS2 123 was one of six bought new in 1929. With the legend 'Limited Stop' mounted across its radiator, it is seen at Nottingham whilst operating the London to Scarborough service in the early 'thirties. Along with its sisters, it was given a new Roe bus body in 1936. (EYMS)

*One of a batch of ten Tilling-bodied 32-seat Tilling Stevens B10A2 buses purchased new by East Yorkshire in 1929, 147 is pictured here on a private hire duty during the early 'thirties. (EYMS)*

*Restimg at Hessle Square in the early 'thirties are 119, a Tilling-bodied Tilling Stevens B10A2 and 135, an all-Leyland TD1 both of which were purchased new in 1929.   (EYMS)*

*This superb view shows 166, a Leyland Lion PLSC1 of 1927 vintage acquired from A.Robinson (Bridlington & District), travelling through Bridlington on a town service in June 1935. Fitted with a large destination board on its front roof dome, above this can be seen an East Yorkshire advert on the end of a building alongside the Chapel which was later demolished to enable the bus station to be extended. (G.H.F.Atkins/EYMS)*

Before this memorable year ended, the company took delivery of its first brand-new buses, five all-Leyland 31-seat PLSCs which had originally been ordered by Lee & Beaulah. Entering service in December, these were to give East Yorkshire ten years valuable service and were the fore-runners of a large Leyland fleet built up in the years prior to World War II.

The first directors' meeting had been held in the offices of Messrs. Buckley, Hall & Delvin on 8 October 1926 and it was at that meeting that Mr.Bee was appointed as the company's chief engineer. It was also agreed that an application be made to the British Automobile Traction Co.Ltd. that East Yorkshire Motor Services be added to the list of B.A.T. Associated Bus Companies and that company's name be put on the passes issued by them to directors and officials of the Hull-based concern. Both applications were readily accepted by B.A.T. and were instituted on 1 January 1927. Surprisingly however, was the fact that although the new company was registered on 5 October, its business was not commenced until three days later.

One of the points under discussion at this first meeting related to the property at Anlaby Common which had been bought by the company and Mr.Harvey was given authorisation to negotiate with the Garden Village development Co. for the purchase of land adjoining the house which at that time was being used as an office, together with any other land which might be available on this site. By November, all the land required had been obtained and plans for its use were put under way before the end of the year.

Mr.John Spencer Wills was appointed company secretary on 15 November 1926 and on this same day, an application was made to the York Hackney Licensing Committee for 20 vehicles to be licensed to run into York to a terminus at Piccadilly. After considering this, York granted licences for 10 vehicles only, this enabling a service to commence from Hull, running via Market Weighton. Seeking further expansion, the feasibility of a service to Scarborough was next to be explored, but due to an agreement between United Automobile Services Ltd. and Harrogate & District Road Car Co. Ltd., whose share of the business - territorially speaking - drew a line from Ripon to the East Coast, passage to Scarborough could not be allowed to east Yorkshire Motor Services Ltd. without crossing this imaginary line. As a result of this, the matter had to be deferred. Determined to seek new avenues of development however, the company applied in December to join the London Provincial Owners Association, obviously with a view to running a service to the capital.

Looking to eliminate more competition from their main operating area, East Yorkshire made offers to two more Hull independents, Newington Motor & Engineering Co.Ltd. and Binningtons, but in both cases were found unacceptable and thus no deals were able to be made.

Although office accommodation was already owned at Anlaby Common, this was now found to be inadequate for the growing company's needs and it was thus decided to rent accommodation in Leyton Chambers in Paragon Street in the heart of the city. Occupation took place on 1 January 1927 and was continued until May 1941 when the property was badly damaged in one of the many bomb attacks made on Hull.

As far as the fleet was concerned, three new motor cycles were purchased for use by the company's inspectors and a Ford model T was selected for conversion into a breakdown lorry, its chassis and body being modified accordingly. One of the main difficulties found in the operation of such a mixed fleet (apart from maintenance and the need for a wide range of spares) was the limited operational range due to many of the buses having small fuel tanks. In an attempt to overcome this problem, estimates were obtained for the purchase of additional petrol tanks and by the end of January 1927 a total of 20 buses had been so fitted at the cost of £10 each. In an attempt to recoup some of this money, discussions took place relating to the idea of adorning the fleet with external advertising posters, but as agreement could not be reached on this matter (some directors feeling that such a move would deface the buses), this was postponed for further consideration at a later date.

At Driffield, land had now been acquired together with a garage for the sum of £775 and before this was put to use, further land was sought in Westgate so that the premises could be gradually extended. Meanwhile, in Hull space was desperately needed for the housing of 30-plus buses and in December 1926 the company managed to purchase Lister Street garage for £4,900. Alterations were soon in hand to extend this property, this costing a further £450.

Despite further attempts to persuade local operators to join 'the big company', East Yorkshire were unsuccessful and, as they wished to quickly build up the size of their fleet to allow new routes to be opened, it was decided to investigate the purchase of several vehicles at that time offered for sale by the B.A.T. at £125 each. Initially an order was placed for 2 of these buses with delivery at the earliest possible date, with an option for a further 6 in May 1927 and 12 more in June. This 'order' was later amended to 6 buses for May delivery and 9 in June but following the arrival of the first 3, which were in much worse condition than had been expected, the remainder were cancelled. The trio taken into stock were open-top Daimler CC-type double deckers dating from 1913, one of which had originally operated for Northern General at Gateshead. Due to the lack of facilities at Hull, all were overhauled and repainted by Birch Bros.,London on behalf of East Yorkshire before travelling northwards.

1927 began with the resignation of Mr.Harvey as manager of East Yorkshire, his replacement being E.J.Lee who took up his new position on the first day of the year. This led to little change in policy however and the proposals drawn up the previous year were totally unaffected by this change 'at the top'. By April 1927 East Yorkshire were operating a total of 16 routes, most of which radiated from Hull. These served Willerby (2 routes); North Cave; Ferriby; Brough; Bridlington; Withernsea (2 routes); Hedon; Sutton (2 routes); Preston and York, the remaining services operating from Driffield to Beverley; Hornsea and Fridaythorpe. Except for the services to York and Fridaythorpe which had been inaugurated by East Yorkshire, all the others were those which had been acquired from the firms brought together under the new company's umbrella. Amongst the development plans drawn up for 1927 were a proposed service from Hull to Hessle via Barrow Lane and one from Driffield to Hornsea. The Hessle Watch Committee however refused to grant a licence for the first mentioned route and it was not until a second appeal had been lodged that consent was finally given. This was for an hourly service operating via Ferriby Road, Tranby Head Lane and Swanland Road. In the meantime, in June, Samuel Binnington asked East Yorkshire to make him an offer for his Hull to Hornsea route together with 2 Leyland buses, and after some deliberation, the company offered £3,500 for this package. Less than amused, Binnington promptly rejected this and the negotiations came to an abrupt end with the latter continuing to operate the service.

The next new buses to arrive did so in 1927. Comprising 11 Leyland-bodied 36-seat rear entrance Leyland PLSC3 Lions, the first five of these had been ordered by Lee & Beaulah prior to the formation of East Yorkshire whilst the remaining six were the first new vehicles to be bought by the infant company. The life of one of these buses - 61 - in its original form was to be very brief however, for after only nine weeks in service it was involved in a serious accident which damaged its body beyond economical repair. After receiving attention, its chassis was despatched to London Lorries who fitted it with a new 33-seat rear entrance body before its eventual return to service.

Throughout the late summer, negotiations had been taking place with Fussey's of Cottingham and Springville Passenger Services of Hessle which resulted in their purchase by East Yorkshire in November 1927.

Thomas Fussey, who traded as 'Executors of Elizabeth Fussey' and later as 'Enterprise' moved to Cottingham from Skirlaugh at the turn of the century and quickly established himself with a horse-cab service in the area. By 1910/1 he had acquired the licences and services of a Mr.Lazenby and ran horse buses from Cottingham to Hull using double deckers. This service continued to operate throughout the great war but was finally discontinued in 1919 when Fussey turned his attention to mechanically-propelled vehicles. His first venture in this field was made with a ten-year old 5-seat Argyl which he started to operate over his former horse bus route on 10 July. As demand grew, so he found the need to operate a larger vehicle and in July 1920 he bought a former War Department Dennis 3-ton lorry chassis and had this fitted with a Barnaby bus body. Seeing there was also a need for smaller vehicles which could be employed on private hire duties, he purchased a pair of Maxwell taxicabs in 1921 and made these available for both taxi and private travel purposes. During the 1922-26 period, Fussey purchased 2 Tilling Stevens TTA1s, 3 Daimler Y-type charabancs, a Crossley and 2 Dennis 4-ton open-top double deckers, some of which replaced his older vehicles and gave him a fleet of 6 buses and 2 taxis by the end of 1926. During the general strike of 1926, Fussey transported Naval personnel to and from Hull Docks and in doing so, struck up a close personal friendship with the captain of the HMS Enterprise. As a result of this, he adopted the fleet name 'Enterprise' in July 1926.

Following the negotiations instigated by East Yorkshire, Fussey finally agreed to sell his solitary route (Cottingham to Hull) to the company together with the 2 Dennis double deckers, 2 Daimler charabancs, his taxi business and 2 taxis and his land and garage at Station Yard, Cottingham for a total of £9,000. Only the 2 Dennis buses were placed in service by East Yorkshire, (the Daimler being immediately resold) and these were transferred to their new owner on 24 November 1927. The taxi business along with the 2 Maxwell taxicabs were quickly resold back to G.Fussey for £150 whilst the land at Cottingham was still owned by East Yorkshire until 1977 despite the garage having been unused by the company from 1936 until its demolition in February 1954. This land then passed to the NBC's property company, Omnibus Estates Ltd. with whom it remained until eventually sold in 1985.

The other operator taken over in November 1927 was Springville Passenger Services, a company formed in 1921 by Thomas Leonard Bell, his son Len, and his uncle under the parent company of Hull Road Motor & Electrical Engineering Co.Ltd. which was loosely connected with flying at Hedon. From a garage situated on Hessle High Road near First Lane, Hessle, one solitary route was operated from Hessle to Hull. The first vehicle owned was a 14-seat Buick converted from an ambulance, this being quickly joined by a 20-seat Garford, 2 Austin 20-seaters and a 14-seat Napier. The service operated to a 15-minute frequency and in order to provide sufficient vehicles with which to maintain this, during 1923 a 14-seat Barnaby-bodied Atlas and 2 Leyland 32-seaters were added to the fleet. Another Leyland arrived in 1924 whilst during the following year a secondhand AEC B-type 30-seater and a former War Department Leyland RAF-type with Barnaby 30-seat bodywork were purchased.

Following a request made to Hessle Watch Committee being granted to allow double deck buses to be operated in their area, Springville purchased 2 secondhand open-top double deck bodies from Binningtons (these having previously been mounted on Straker Squire chassis) early in 1927 and fitted them to their Leyland S-type chassis. The single deck bodies removed from these were placed in store and ultimately passed to East Yorkshire together with the Springville business, 6 vehicles and the Hull - Hessle service on 24 November 1927. The purchase price was £8,000 but did not include the garage which was retained by Hull Road Motor & Electrical Engineering Co. Ltd.

During November 1927, East Yorkshire converted 8 of their double deckers from solid to pneumatic tyres at a total cost of £401 and, still seeking additional vehicles approached Harrogate & District Road Car Co.Ltd. with a view to purchasing three Leylands from them. After failing to agree a price, this plan was dropped and instead the directors gave permission for an additional three new vehicles to be ordered for delivery in 1928. Finally, just before the close of the year J.W.Smith of Selby offered his 'Imperial' company to East Yorkshire, but this was rejected due to being thought to be too far away from the company's main operating area.

1928 witnessed the arrival of no fewer than 43 brand new vehicles, all of which were bus-bodied single deckers. These comprised 6 Chevrolet 14/17 seaters, 20 Leyland-bodied 32-seat rear entrance Leyland PLSC3s, 16 Tilling-bodied 32-seat Tilling Stevens B10A2s and a 40-seat Guy FCX. The Chevrolets and Guy had been ordered by Jackson of Aldborough before that company's takeover by East Yorkshire on 2 May 1928.

The origins of Jacksons Motors dated back to October 1920 when Frank and Walter Jackson obtained licences to drive a lorry owned by their father who was a brewer and maltster. Later, in February 1922 the two brothers decided to venture forth on their own and applied for a licence to operate a bus service from Aldborough to Hull via Sproatley. As their father had by this time sold his business, he presented them with his lorry - a model T Ford - and it was this that was first used on the new service. To make it suitable for the carriage of passengers, bench seats were fitted and access was gained by steps at the rear. Initially, only one journey in each direction was operated daily, but later in 1922 this was doubled to two return journeys, this becoming the 'normal' service. When their only competitor over these roads (a Mr.Collinson) discontinued his operations which were known to the local inhabitants as 'Tankards Bus' in the autumn of 1922 - this being one of the last horse-buses in Hull - a second Ford T was purchased, this having a Baico extension and being fitted with a 20-seat charabanc body. The service was then extended to Aldborough Cliffs, the Hull terminus being at Cleveland Street, Witham, and six runs were operated each Saturday. As passenger loadings increased, it soon became obvious that a third - and larger - vehicle was needed and so in January 1924 Jacksons purchased a 26-seat 2-ton Vulcan which on its first journey carried not 26 passengers, but 52 ! In April of the following year a second Vulcan arrived, as did a 26-seat Barnaby-bodied Guy BA, these allowing the original 'lorry-bus' to be withdrawn. Three months later, in July 1925 an AEC 202-type 26/30-seat charabanc was added to the fleet and despite competition from Anlaby Motor Bus Co., Jackson's growth and good fortunes continued. In November 1925 the company was granted a licence from Smeaton Street, Hull to Hornsea via Mappleton and Aldborough - a service at one time operated by Binningtons - and during 1926 further services were introduced, interconnecting the Hull - Aldborough route with one from Aldborough to Withernsea. To operate these, 2 more Guy BBs and a Guy B were purchased in 1926 with a further Guy BB, a 14-seat 1-ton Morris and a 14-seat Chevrolet LM joining the fleet in 1927.

Seeing the dramatic increase in the use of private cars, towards the end of 1927 Jacksons began to think about selling their business and to this end started talks with East Yorkshire who were obviously extremely interested. A deal was reached early in 1928 when East Yorkshire agreed a price of £10,000 for Jacksons' 8 milk chocolate & white liveried buses and three routes.

The other operator taken over in 1928 was John Charles Holt, licencee of the Turks Head Inn at Newport since 1919. Deciding to enter the transport field in 1921, Holt purchased a secondhand 13-seat model T Ford and began operating a service from Newport to Hull. Such was the success of his new venture that during the next three years he added 2 more secondhand and a new Ford T to his fleet as well as purchasing a secondhand Atlas and a similar-aged Garford. Despite his service being well patronised, Holt was continually refused any extensions from June 1923 to mid-1924 as a result of objections lodged by Lee & Beaulah and thus any ideas of expansion in this direction were quickly shattered. This led Holt to start to concentrate more heavily on private hire work and when he sold his Newport - Hull service to East Yorkshire for £500 in May 1928, he retained all his vehicles for further use. Since that date, Holt built up an initially extremely successful coaching business and in more recent times took over Danbys Coaches of Sutton on Hull in addition to starting an express service from Newport to Beverley and one from Newport to Goole and gaining several lucrative schools contracts. After starting services to South Hunsley Comprehensive School near Welton in 1983, which competed directly with journeys provided by East Yorkshire, Holt got into difficulties and ceased running coaches and buses during the late 'eighties.

Having further consolidated their position by the acquisition of Jacksons and Holt, East Yorkshire found that one of their former inspectors, Walter Baines became a thorn in their side when he started up in opposition under the title of 'Driffield & District Services', competing with the 'big' company over the Driffield section of their Hull - Bridlington route. In addition, he had opened up a new service from Langtoft to Driffield and although East Yorkshire were in a position to take trade from him with duplicate vehicles etc., the residents of Langtoft remained loyal to Baines and allowed E.Y.M.S. buses to pass them at stops along the route. Following numerous attempts to persuade him to sell out - each of which Baines refused - East Yorkshire finally increased their frequency over his routes to such an extent that in 1928 they forced him into liquidation. Other operators sought by East Yorkshire (Sharpes of Hedon; Everingham Bros. of Pocklington and Binningtons of Hull) all refused their offers and remained independent. Binningtons had been approached previously without success and so desperate were East Yorkshire to acquire this company that they offered Sam Binnington a seat on the board of directors plus a part cash/part share in Binningtons offer with a promise that Binningtons would be operated as a subsidiary, thus giving Sam Binnington a major share of the control of his business. This remarkable offer also failed to persuade him to sell !

Looking for ways to encourage more people to travel on their services, East Yorkshire advertised their first 'Cheap Fares Weeks' during 1928, these being planned for the summer season, and additionally supplied 2,000 framed route maps to various hotels within their operating area in order to publicise the routes worked. In anticipation of the opening of Boothferry Bridge, the company applied to the Hull Watch Committee to operate via this new structure from Hull to Goole, but this was refused.

Seeking premises in Scarborough where buses could be accommodated overnight, East Yorkshire in September 1928 took out a ten-year lease on a garage owned by Robinson's Motors Ltd. in Vine Street. Being larger than they themselves required, and knowing that West Yorkshire Road Car Co.Ltd. were also at that time seeking premises in Scarborough, East Yorkshire signed an agreement on 24 September with the latter company which allowed them part use of the garage for the duration of the lease. Although East Yorkshire gained an option to purchase this property upon expiry of the lease, this as will be seen later, was not taken up.

Two months later, in November 1928 the authorised share

capital in East Yorkshire was increased from £125,000 (to which it had been increased in December 1927) to £160,000.

Following a letter to the company from the Chief Constable of Hull regarding passenger safety on public service vehicles, 120 first-aid kits were purchased for fitting to each bus in the fleet. Similarly, 5 vehicles were fitted with emergency exits to enable the acquisition of further licences for the Leeds services.

Being keen to expand their operations to include long distance services, Mr.E.J.Lee in November 1928 together with a representative of the Barnsley & District Traction Co.Ltd. negotiated the purchase of Bennetts of Askern for a sum in the region of £20,000, realising that later, in the operating of the Yorkshire Services Pool, such operator's long distance routes would be of great value.

Nearer home, proposals were put to Hull City Tramways Committee concerning the joint operation of some services within the city boundary. These were rejected by Hull by six votes to four and although it was proposed to start new discussions in June of the following year, it was not until October 1931 that these finally got under way.

Having now become firmly established, East Yorkshire were anxious to reach agreements with other major operators in order to establish longer routes to places outside their original territory, and in January 1929 they held talks with both Yorkshire Traction and United to this end. A draft territorial agreement was proposed between themselves and United to allow them to run north of Dotterill and during the same month, terms were finalised with Yorkshire Traction for a route from Hull into their territory at Doncaster. It was agreed that all receipts from the section between Doncaster and Goole would be paid to Yorkshire Traction with those between Goole and Hull going to East Yorkshire. Similarly, on Traction's service from Doncaster to York, East Yorkshire would receive the takings from the Selby to York section.

# FURTHER EXPANSION & CONSOLIDATION

The search for further expansion and consolidation continued and offers were made to two Bridlington operators, Archer Robinson and the Blue Bus Company, but both fell short of the figure these independents expected to receive and neither could be persuaded to sell at this time.

New vehicles to enter the fleet in 1929 comprised 10 Tilling Stevens B10A2s with Tilling 32-seat rear entrance bus bodywork, 6 Hall Lewis-bodied 25-seat rear entrance Leyland TS2 luxury coaches and 10 lowbridge all-Leyland Titan TD1s with open rear staircases. These were the first new double deckers to be purchased by the company and the first five entered service in February. Although four more Leyland TS2 coaches had been ordered by East Yorkshire, these never took their place in the fleet and were instead diverted upon delivery to Eastern Counties Omnibus Co.Ltd. of Norwich.

On 17 May a new express service was inaugurated from Hull to Blackpool whilst during the following month a service was opened from Hull to Newcastle upon Tyne. Both of these, together with a new Birmingham service were maintained by the new Tiger coaches and at least one of these was fitted with a toilet compartment. These vehicles were operated from the new depot in Anlaby Road, Hull, 7.528 square yards in area and bought for £9,000, which had been opened in May 1929 and which replaced the much smaller Lister Street premises. Following the move, the now vacant Lister Street depot was leased to Hull Corporation Tramways, the lease being dated to commence in June.

Throughout the summer, few changes of importance took place and it was not until the closing months of the year that any further development was witnessed. Following approaches made by Baileys Bus Service of Wilberfoss and Thompsons of York - both of whom wished to sell to East Yorkshire, but neither of which were purchased - the company secretary was instructed to negotiate with United Automobile Services in order to gain a portion of the 'carve-up' of Bridlington & District and Scarborough & District Motor Services.

Originally named 'Robinsons Motors' by its owner, Archer Robinson, the title 'Bridlington & District' was adopted in 1923. Born on 18 September 1873, Archer Robinson became a self-taught mechanic and began his first bus service as early as May 1905 with a single-cylinder Napier fitted with a wooden body. This had been built by his father (who by trade was a cabinet maker) and incorporated seating for 10 passengers. His first service was from Bridlington to North Landing via Flamborough and as this gained in popularity, a second vehicle was purchased. This, a 30-seat De-Launey Belleville, made its debut in May 1907 and was later rebodied as a 'torpedo' charabanc. Further expansion was slow and the Napier was withdrawn in 1908 and placed in store (where it remained until 1924 !). By 1913 however, a Darracq Landaulette taxicab had been purchased and with this Robinson began operating private hire trips to places as far afield as Whitby and the Goathland Moors. Shortly before the outbreak of World War I, a second De-Launey Belleville charabanc was purchased, but before it could start to earn revenue it, along with its sister vehicle was commandeered by the War Department and Archer Robinson himself joined the armed forces, serving in the Transport Regiment.

Demobbed early in 1919, he returned to the transport scene in Bridlington from an address at 3, Ashbourne Avenue, his first vehicles being a pair of 40hp Dennis charabancs, the chassis of which he bought at Government sales. The bodies for these were built by Pickerings of Beverley (who built bodies for subsequent Robinson vehicles too) and had seating for 25/30 passengers. Two more Dennis' were acquired in 1920 followed by 3 Lancias in 1921 and a Lancia and an AEC Y-type in 1922.

Vacating his original Portland Place garage in 1921, he moved into a garage in Cliff Street where a booking office was quickly established to cope with his growing excursion work. Still maintaining his service to Flamborough, a 'branch' was added to serve Thornwick Bay where Robinson had built a cafe and had opened a camping site etc. The fleet was further expanded in 1923 with the purchase of yet another Lancia and a Daimler, the latter having 20-seat bodywork by

*Right : Primitive lifting gear has been assembled to aid the recovery of 1929 Leyland TD1 135 after it had 'left the road' at Hutton Cranswick in September 1931. (EYMS)*

*Below : One of a pair of all-Leyland LT1s acquired with the business of A.Robinson (Bridlington & District) in 1929, 167 is seen here in 1943 complete with wartime white wing tips and guard rails after being returned from loan to Crosville Motor Services. It never re-entered service with East Yorkshire and was sold in 1946. (EYMS)*

*New to Burn of Withernsea in 1926, Leyland Lioness PLC1 BT9981 passed to Blue Bus Service, Bridlington (in whose livery it is seen here) in 1927 before being acquired by East Yorkshire some three years later.*

United of Lowestoft, and two more vehicles - a Lancia and a Daimler - were added in 1924. A new service from Promenade Corner, Bridlington to Gordon Street in the Old Town was inaugurated on 21 July 1924 and upon hearing that another Bridlington firm, Tooth & Waddington were experiencing financial difficulties, Robinson opened talks with a view to taking them over, which he ultimately did on 6 January 1925.

Tooth & Robinson had opened a new motor garage in Prospect Street, Bridlington under the name of Trown, Tooth & Twentyman in 1922 and soon afterwards began operating buses under the title 'The Red Buses', using two single deckers on a service along Bridlington's sea-front. Trown and Twentyman left the company in1923 and were replaced by H.L.Waddington, and at this same time the Prospect Street premises were sold and a new bus garage opened under the name of 'Parade Motor Station'. Additional buses bought were a Leyland double decker, an AEC K-type double decker and a Maxwell charabanc and with these, a second

route was opened, this running to Flamborough. Two circular town services were inaugurated as in 1924 was a new route from Bridlington to Driffield and 2 Leyland 50-seat toastracks were purchased in May 1924 for the new circular operations.

An interesting departure for Tooth & Waddington in 1923 was when they hired two buses to Hull City Transport. The latter, who at that time were short of motor buses, planned a new route from Hull to Newbridge Road and used Tooth & Waddington's Leyland double decker and AEC Y-type single decker - complete with the Bridlington company's drivers - on this new service. Although after a few months both buses were returned to their rightful owner, the two drivers opted to remain with Hull Corporation, one later becoming an inspector with that undertaking.

*An assortment of East Yorkshire vehicles can be seen in this 1932 view of the company's depot in Cliff Street, Bridlington which was acquired with the business of A.Robinson (Bridlington & District) in 1929. (EYMS)*

*Newington's Crossley L6519 rests at Hornsea in the company of Blue Bus Service GMC BT8470 in 1926.*

*Although AT8961, a 14-seat Barnaby charabanc-bodied Crossley PN, passed to East Yorkshire with the Hull City Motor Works (Kingston) fleet in 1932, it was not used by its new owners and was instead quickly sold. It was new in 1924 to Newington of Hull in whose livery it is seen here.*

*Wakefields Motor Services Crossley BT6826 passed to Hull City Motor Works along with the Wakefield business in 1925. In this picture, the white ribbons above its bonnet appear to signify that it was being used on a private hire duty in connection with a wedding.*

*AT5732, a 29-seat bus-bodied Commer 3P of Hull City Motor Works was acquired by them from Hull Corporation in 1923 having been supplied new to J.B.McMaster of Hull in 1921.*

*Resting at Nottingham on its way from London to Scarborough in 1935 is 187, a coach-seated E.C.O.C.-bodied Leyland TS4 which was purchased new in 1932. (EYMS)*

*Another former Newington vehicle to pass to Hull City Motor Works (Kingston) and thence to East Yorkshire was KH1945, a Maudslay ML3B of 1926 vintage. Numbered 195 by East Yorkshire, it gave little service however and was withdrawn in September 1932.*

As none of Robinson's services operated on Sundays, this let in another operator, J.H.Aitken, a taxi proprietor who was keen to establish himself in the Bridlington area. Entering the bus business in April 1925 with a secondhand 14-seat Atlas, he began running between Bridlington and Flamborough from a garage at John Halls Mews, Flamborough not only on Sundays, but seven days a week. Soon afterwards a garage was acquired in Queen Street, Bridlington and during 1925 a trio of 18-seat GMC K16s and a 14-seat Chevrolet were purchased. These were employed on the new services opened to Hornsea, Scarborough and Driffield and following this, the Flamborough service was extended in Bridlington from Queen Street to Belvedere. Operating under the title of 'Blue Bus Services', expansion was rapid and during 1926 no fewer than 9 additional vehicles were purchased - these being of mixed parentage and with no attempt towards standarisation. These comprised 3 Chevrolets; 1 Daimler CM; 1 Leyland Leveret; 1 GMC K14; 1 Reo and 1 Overland all bought new and a Leyland N-type double decker acquired secondhand from Sheffield Corporation. Another dramatic increase in the size of Aitken's fleet was witnessed in 1927 when 7 secondhand and 3 new single deckers of Chevrolet; Albion; Leyland and Vulcan manufacture were acquired,

*Right : Numbered 43 in the Kingston fleet, United-bodied Gilford 166OT KH9297 passed to East Yorkshire in 1932 with the Hull City Motor Works (Kingston) business. Given fleet number 203 by its new owner, it remained in service until 1934.*

*Below : This Straker Squire double decker - BT394 - began life with Binningtons in 1920 and after serving them for four years was sold to Hull City Tramways for whom it operated until 1933.*

*Straker Squire A-type double decker BT4802 was purchased new by Binningtons in 1922 and remained in service until 1926. It is seen here operating the Hull to Hornsea service carrying superb period advertising posters along its upper deck side panels.*

bringing the total operated to 23. Following this fleet expansion, it was not surprising that Blue Bus sought new services and in January 1928 an application was made for a route from Bridlington to Leeds via Malton and York. This was granted and in July a pair of 35-seat Leyland PLSCs were purchased for its operation. Also added to the fleet at this same time was a secondhand Straker Squire double decker which was needed for the well-patronised Flamborough service. In May 1928, in order to be able to inject more finance into the business, Aitken took a Mr.Kaye into partnership and the company was then re-formed as 'Blue Bus Services (Bridlington) Ltd.'

The last major development took place in November 1929 when Blue Bus applied for licences to operate between Bridlington and Manchester via Huddersfield; to Scarborough via Driffield and Beverley; to Newcastle upon Tyne via Whitby and to North Burton via Rudston. These were all granted and the new operations commenced immediately.

Following this sudden widening of the company's area of operation, it came as something of a surprise when in January 1930 Blue Bus announced that it was to merge with Scarborough & District Motor Services Ltd. who, since October 1929 had been under the management control of United Automobile Services.

During the discussions between United and East Yorkshire which resulted in the latter acquiring much of Robinsons business, it was also agreed that East Yorkshire should take the Bridlington operations acquired from Blue Bus Services and thus, in May 1930 the assets of Blue Bus were divided between United, West Yorkshire and East Yorkshire, the latter gaining most services and 17 vehicles. Two months earlier, perhaps in anticipation of gaining a major foothold in Bridlington, East Yorkshire had purchased a garage in Havelock Crescent which was, in October, supplemented by

the Cliff Street garage leased from Archer Robinson who had retained this since the sale of his company.

Returning to Robinson, April 1925 had seen him open up services to Driffield, Hornsea and Bempton and in 1926 he had started a regular service to Scarborough, these like his others only operating six days a week. During August of that year, the Watch Committee issued an ultimatum - operate seven days a week or lose your licences - and as a result, and much to his personal disagreement, Robinson had to accept these new terms. Although his stage carriage services were all well patronised, excursion work continued to play a major role in his company's activities and unusually, Robinson advertised 'Money refunded before start if wet'. By now, garage space was also rented at Flamborough whilst in Bridlington the fleet was housed at Cliff Street garage, Portland Place and the Esplanade. During the winter months when fewer vehicles were required to maintain his various operations, some buses were laid up in what was Arthur Knaggs Mews.

Around 1928/9 a new service was started from Bridlington to Leeds and by this time the fleet had been increased yet again with the purchase of 2 Leyland PLSC1s, 6 ADCs and 2 Leyland LT1s. Soon afterwards, Archer Robinson decided to sell out and began negotiations not with East Yorkshire, but with United. These were successfully concluded and Robinson ceased operations on 30 September 1929 when United took over his operations and 10 ex.Bridlington &

District buses until agreement had been reached with East Yorkshire as to their involvement. This being reached, East Yorkshire acquired - from United - 8 of the former Bridlington & District buses and took over operations on 13 January 1930.

During the final month of the previous year, the London & North Eastern Railway Company was ceded an interest in East Yorkshire Motor Services Ltd. equal to that of Tilling and British Automobile Traction Co.Ltd.

1930 witnessed the arrival of more new double deck buses for East Yorkshire - 6 lowbridge-bodied all-Leyland Titan TD1s with open rear staircases - and 5 more coaches (a trio of Ransome-bodied 26-seat Leyland TS2s and a pair of Leyland LT1s fitted with 26-seat bodies by London Lorries. Later in the year, in October, Sidney & Erwin Everingham of Pocklington offered their very lucrative business to the company for £25,000, and much as East Yorkshire would

have liked to acquire this business, they were unable to take up the offer due to financial reasons. The cause of these was the fact that some weeks earlier they had applied for 1,000 £1 shares in London Coastal Coaches, although this was trimmed to 500 shares in November. The only other development of note during 1930 was the agreeing of terms with West Yorkshire Road Car Co.Ltd. on 19 November for the joint use of the latter's bus station and cafe facilities etc. at Wellington Street, Leeds.

The following year turned out to be one of the least eventful in the whole of the company's history with no new vehicles delivered and no further operators acquired. Towards the end of the summer, negotiations took place with Hull Corporation Transport regarding the Hull to Sutton service and this was ultimately sold for £3,000 to the municipal undertaking who took over its operation on 2 November.

At head office R.H.Maxwell was made joint manager from 1 May and S.Tilling resigned as a director on that same date. Two months earlier, C.Rawling had replaced John Spencer Wills (now Sir J.S.Wills) as company secretary. Yet another director who left the company during 1930 was Herbert A. Harvey who retired in November. It will be recalled that Mr.Harvey along with E.J.Lee had helped to formulate the policies and organise the purchase of the primary companies during the formation of East Yorkshire some years earlier. Before retiring, one of H.A.Harvey's last major duties was to

supervise the negotiations with Hull City Motor Works with a view to purchasing this sizeable operator. As things transpired, he ended his service with the company before this matter was completed, although it must be recorded that he did much of the spadework which ultimately led to this deal being successfully accomplished.

Established in 1905 by a Mr.Atkinson, Hull City Garage was set up as auto engineers, car body makers and car sales and was managed by employees of Colonel M. Thackwell and Major Upton. After rising to become Hull's leading garage, the company decided to branch out into the field of passenger transport and on 14 January 1920 applied to East Riding County Council for permission for two vehicles to ply on their roads. This was duly granted and in February 1920 two charabancs - a Palladium and a Garford - were licensed for this purpose. On 17 January 1923 the company's name was changed to Hull City Motor Works Ltd. and the trading name 'Kingston Motors' was adopted. During this period, J.B.McMaster, another Hull bus operator had been negotiating with Hull Corporation for the sale of their Hull - Hessle Square service which originated from Owbridge and dated back to 1870. Owing to the service running in part outside the city boundary where the Corporation were unable to operate, they put the licence and 6 vehicles up for tender. That of £4,000 submitted by Hull City Motor Works was accepted and shortly before Easter 1923, they began operations to Hessle using McMaster's former vehicles - a Daimler CK and 5 Commers of varying types. McMaster had been in liason with a draper by the name of John Wardell who, in February 1919 had bought out F.Owbridge of Hessle. McMaster and Wardell has a Humber taxi which was jointly licensed and by 14 December 1919 they were trading under the name 'Hessle Motor Bus Co.'. The two men split up by mid-1920 and through a third party McMaster acquired Wardell's buses. McMaster after the sale of his stage carriage licence continued as a coach operator and only in the last decade did he sell out to Cherry of Beverley.

Towards the end of 1923 Hull City Motor Works applied for a second licence from Hull to Hessle via Anlaby, Willerby and Cottingham, but this was refused as was an application in November 1924 for a service from Hull to Beverley. In an attempt to gain additional licences, they then purchased the business of George W. Tullock on 24 November, this giving them services from Osbourne Street to Dairycoates, Osbourne Street to Hessle Square, Hull to Cottingham via two different routes and Hull to Raywell Sanitorium and adding a further 7 vehicles to their fleet.

George Tullock lived in Bean Street, Hull and owned a wine & spirits warehouse and shop in Regent Street. Seeking an additional source of income, and seeing that there was no tramway service on Sundays until 1.00pm, he decided to provide the local inhabitants with transport and purchased a horse-drawn wagonette. Following the vogue in 1921 he replaced this with a 30cwt Oldsmobile, the chassis of which he bought new and fitted with an old tram body which he suitably modified as a 14-seater. A second Oldsmobile - again fitted with a modified tram body - was purchased in January 1922, this being joined by a Traffic in April and a Vulcan in May. During the period 1922-4 he expanded by opening up the services later taken over by Hull City Motor Works and added to his fleet another Vulcan, a 45hp. Caledon, 4 AEC Y-types and an Austin taxi. An unusual feature of his operations was the semi-OMO working of his Cottingham services. Most of the passengers on these routes were picked up between Cottingham and Newland Avenue, with few joining between the latter point and the Hull's city centre and as a result of this, a conductor would only be used on the first part of the journey, alighting at Newland Avenue to join the next vehicle back to Cottingham. On the remaining section of the route the driver would collect the fares. From January 1922 Tullock used the fleet name 'Swift Motor Bus Service' and most vehicles were then given the names of birds - i.e. Swift; Swallow; Snipe; Eagle; Hawk etc.

By acquiring Tullock's business, Kingston Motors (Hull City Motor Works) had gained the extra licences they needed and

had also increased the size of their fleet. Just as their new operations began to settle down, they learned that Wakefields Motor Services of Walkington were experiencing difficulties following the refusal by the Watch Committee of certain licence applications. An approach was quickly made, and Wakefields business was purchased by Kingston in June 1925.

Shortly after the Great War had ended, the Wakefield family - two sons and a daughter - had started a bus service from Beverley to Bishopburton and later, in May 1922 had begun operations from Walkington to Hull. Operating a mixed fleet of maroon & primrose-liveried Ford T, Vulcan, Crossley and Daimler single deckers, a third service was inaugurated from Beverley to Hornsea via Leven and Catwick and around this same time, following the death of Mr.Wakefield (senior), W.B.Hopkin was made a partner in the business. Hopkin had previously married into the Wakefield family while one of Wakefield's sons, Albine (Duggie) married Gracie Fields' sister.

With Wakefields' licences came 6 vehicles, giving Kingston Motors yet another foothold in an area already served by other operators. Having been given permission to run double deck buses to Brough, Kingston purchased 2 secondhand Thornycroft J-types with 50-seat Dodson bodywork from a London operator, Shamrock Motor Co., placing them in service in February 1926. 3 Crossley single deckers and a Leyland A13 were also added to the fleet in this same year while in 1927, a pair of Guy FBB saloons were purchased. In 1928 a major vehicle replacement programme was embarked upon in an attempt to modernise the fleet and 8 single deckers - 2 Leyland PLSC3s; 2 Chevrolets; 2 Crossleys, an ADC 416 and an Overland - were bought for this purpose. Meanwhile, Kingston Motors who, since November 1926, had operated a wholly-owned subsidiary under the title of Newington Motor & Engineering Co.Ltd. totally absorbed this in 1929. The Newington business had been started in January 1920 by Louis J. Stuart who bought a Maudslay charabanc for private hire work. Four months later, he obtained a licence to run a service from Hull to Beverley and soon afterwards opened a depot in Beverley to supplement his original premises at 53 Walton Street, Hull and additionally eliminate much dead mileage. In 1922 he acquired a licence from J.Pocklington for a service to Hornsea, knowing that this would give him powers to run a circular route covering Beverley, Brandesburton, Hornsea and Ellerby, and after increasing his fleet by the addition of a Crossley, 2 Daimlers and a Thornycroft, he obtained a small garage at Brandesburton where he was able to keep one bus. 1923 saw the arrival of 5 more Crossleys and another Daimler and following the extension of the Brandesburton service to Beeford, this was further extended to Bridlington causing the North Eastern Railway with whom Newington had been competing to sell them their Beeford to Beverley licence. In November 1924 Stuart was offered the revoked licence of Walter Moxon following complaints against Moxon for failing to run his 'Old French Chara' for people who had paid for their return journey from Hull to Beverley. The vehicle referred to was a 30-seat De Dion Bouton.

Sadly, in 1926 Louis Stuart died. His son Arthur then took over the running of the Newington business, but as a result of his lack of experience in bus operation (although he was a qualified engineer), he sold the business, licences and vehicles in November 1926 to Hull City Motor Works who operated it as a wholly-owned subsidiary. In June 1928 the operations of William 'Billy' Hayton were acquired, despite the fact that he had refused to sell to Harvey at an earlier date, and in addition to his licence, Hull City Motor Works also took over his 2 Chevrolets which had probably been ordered in anticipation of this sale.

Following the absorption of Newington in 1929, Kingston Motors increased their fleet yet again with 12 vehicles arriving in 1929 (4 Manchesters; 2 Overlands; 4 Gilford 166OTs, an AEC 426 and a secondhand Dennis double decker acquired from Pickwick of London), 2 in 1930 (a Gilford 168OT and a Leyland TD1) and 3 more Gilfords in 1931, the latter arriving shortly before talks opened with East

Yorkshire which were subsequently to lead to their purchase of the company. Agreement was reached between the two parties in December 1931 although it took until 16 April of the following year before details of the transfer of shares etc. could be sorted out. The agreement stated that the title of 'Kingston Motors' was to be retained and that the company would be operated as a wholly-owned subsidiary of East Yorkshire but under the control of T.B.A.T. with joint managership. Kingston's manager at that time was J.Maxwell and as a result of the terms of the takeover, he then became joint manager with the General manager of East Yorkshire Motor Services. A document was drawn up governing the hire of Kingston vehicles to East Yorskhire after which all the vehicles in the Kingston fleet were adorned with stickers proclaiming 'On Hire to EYMS'. Kingston Motors' maroon & cream livery and fleet name were retained and a total of 22 buses were involved in the deal.

Whilst negotiations relating to the acquisition of Kingston Motors were underway, talks had also been started with Binningtons in a renewed attempt to bring them into the East Yorkshire fold following several earlier unsuccessful approaches. Samuel Binnington, on marrying a Miss Palphraman at around the turn of the century, took over the operation of her father's horse-bus service between Kirkella and Hull. In addition to carrying passengers, a service was also provided for the transportation of goods including fruit, foodstuffs, coal and laundry, but this was soon discontinued as the passenger business grew. After becoming well established, Samuel Binnington turned his attention towards motor vehicles and in June 1912 applied for a licence to run 2 motor buses over his horse-bus routes. This was granted and a pair of 23-seat Lacres were acquired on the last day of July. Early the following year 2 Commer WP1 buses were bought and during the 1914-18 period a further Commer was obtained, this being an RC-type. Increasing the frequency of his service following the return of peace. Binnington added 2 more Commers, a Barnaby-bodied Palladium and a Straker Squire double decker to his growing fleet, the latter arriving on 15 March 1920. Seeking further expansion, a new service was started in 1922 from Hull to Hornsea with two sleeve-valve Daimler Y-type single deckers and one of his old chain-driven Commers. The route taken was via Coniston, Skirlaugh and Leven and the service was augumented by unlicensed runs to Aldborough Cliffs whenever there were sufficient passengers to justify this. After complaints from Anlaby Motor Bus Co. however, Binnington was forced to make a licence application for this extension, and not surprisingly this was refused in June 1923. It was at this juncture amusing to note that whilst Binnington was 'illegally' operating to Aldborough Cliffs, the Straker Squire double decker was despatched to make the last run from the Cliffs at 9.30pm one evening and upon arrival it was found that no fewer than 126 passengers needed to be transported. Despite the bus only being a 52-seater, all 126 passengers were squeezed aboard and somehow the conductor managed to collect every fare !

Binningtons became a limited company in October 1923 and soon afterwards started a new service from Willerby to Skidby via Cottingham and purchased a trio of 14-seat Lancias for this new operation. By 1925 the Hornsea to Hull service had been extended to run through to Hessle and a new garage was opened at Cliff Road, Hornsea to supplement the original premises at Carr Lane, Willerby. With the opening of the new Willerby/Kingston road in 1926, a licence was granted to operate from Willerby to Hull via this more direct route and this immediately proved popular with passengers. By now, the fleet was becoming old and expensive to maintain and so plans were made for a massive replacement programme. During 1925 a Leyland C9 charabanc and 2 Leyland LB5-type double deckers made their debut and during the following year no fewer than 4 Leyland PLSC1s were purchased. 7 more PLSCs arrived in 1927/8 along with another LB5-type double decker and these allowed the withdrawal of several older members of the fleet.

By 1928 the company had outgrown their Hornsea garage and so alternative premises were sought. These were found further along Cliff Road and consisted of a picture house/dance hall which were both purchased and altered to make them suitable for housing buses. Upon completion of this work the original garage was closed and the new one brought into full use.

1929 saw the arrival of 3 new Leyland LT1s and a TS2 which were joined by 2 more TS2s in the following year. All carried Leyland front-entrance bus bodywork. A further service was started in 1930 from Willerby to the De La Pole Mental Hospital although being solely for the benefit of visitors, it only operated on a limited number of occasions each week. By far the most striking development was however an order placed for 3 new closed-top double deck buses which materialised in 1931 as Leyland TD1s with Leyland highbridge bodywork. These were allocated to Hornsea garage due to their height preventing their passage under Willerby bridge. The success of these new arrivals led the company to order a further 3 for delivery in 1932, although these were of Leyland's TD2 type and had Strachan highbridge bodies. These, like their sisters also had to be allocated to Hornsea garage. Although these proved to be the last vehicles to be purchased by Binningtons, an oil-engined, Park Royal-bodied AEC Regent demonstrator was borrowed in 1932 for trials on the Hull to Hornsea via Skirlaugh route. Had Binnington Motors Ltd. continued in business independently, it is possible that vehicles of the latter type may well have been included in future orders.

The talks started with East Yorkshire towards the end of 1931 turned out to be somewhat protracted, but eventually agreement was reached for East Yorkshire to purchase all Binnington's shares and to operate the company as a wholly-owned subsidiary. The final day of Binnington's operations was 31 December 1932 and on the following morning East Yorkshire took over all their services, their Hornsea depot and 25 vehicles. East Yorkshire had at last succeeded in acquiring the business they had wanted so badly for so long !

East Yorkshire themselves had only a small intake of new vehicles during 1932, these comprising 6 Leyland TS4's with 30-seat rear entrance bus bodied built by Eastern Counties Omnibus Company and 4 all-Leyland lowbridge-bodied Titan TD2 double deckers.

*One of four all-Leyland lowbridge TD2s purchased new in 1932, ornately lined-out 191 is pictured here before its entry into service at Hull.    (Leyland)*

No new vehicles were purchased in 1933, although one of the TD2 double deckers (194) suffered serious damage in an accident in April which resulted in it having to be fitted with a new 52-seat lowbridge body by ECOC. Operationally however, the company continued to expand and on 21 March 500 shares were purchased in the Fawdon Bus Co.Ltd. of Newcastle upon Tyne, a company involved in long distance limited stop operations, for the sum of £536.0.10d. On this same day a share was purchased of Hale Garage & Coachways of London and included with this was one of Hale's Dennis coaches. This however was not taken into stock and was instead passed to West Yorkshire Road Car Co.Ltd. who had conducted both the above transactions on behalf of East Yorkshire and several other companies.

Upon hearing that the business of R.H.Sherwood of Hornsea was for sale, East Yorkshire immediately made an approach with a view to snapping this up. Their objective was achieved on 7 June and Sherwood's operations and fleet were straightaway absorbed. After being concerned with horse-drawn vehicles and taking over Rose Carr, Sherwoods Garage diversified into motor bus operation in 1921 soon after acquiring two motor taxicabs. Their first vehicle, a Ford model-T with Chapmans of Hull charabanc bodywork was used exclusively for private hire work and it was not until November 1925 that the firm made an entry into stage carriage operation. Their route was a local town service which enroute called at Hornsea railway station and was operated by a 14-seat Maxwell. After gaining experience on this, a second route was inaugurated, running from Hornsea to Beverley and was followed by one from Brandesburton to Beverley and to maintain these, 7 Chevrolet single deckers were purchased between 1926 and 1930. Seeking further expansion, a licence was sought for a route from Hull to Hornsea, and following its refusal no more applications were made. The final buses to join the fleet were both acquired secondhand, these being a 14-seat Chevrolet and a 24-seat Reo. After selling their bus interests to East Yorkshire, Sherwoods continued in business from their Newbegin Garage, Hornsea as motor repairers and taxicab operators.

Despite their involvement in operational expansion throughout the year, the company continued to keep a watchful eye on its properties and in 1933 bought a house in Arnold Street, Hull adjacent to their Anlaby Road garage. At Elloughton the land freehold held by J.C.Beaulah was purchased in November 1933 to give East Yorkshire full control of the site whilst in June the former Hull City Motor Works garage on Beverley Road was sold to E.K.Wilson & Son for £5,300.

A major - and revolutionary - development undertaken in 1933 was the inauguration in April of an Air Ferry service from Brough to Immingham in conjunction with the Blackburn Aircraft Company. This involved East Yorkshire providing road transport to Brough aerodrome and for this, the ex.Sherwood 6-cylinder Chevrolet limousine was used, this being fitted with a roof-mounted board to publicise the service.

On 1 December, R.T.Ebrey was appointed General Manager of the company, his predecessor E.J.Lee being elevated to the position of Resident Manager. At this same time R.H.Maxwell was offered the position of Assistant to the General Manager, and accepting this he assumed his duties with immediate effect. Following these managerial changes, a decision was taken to liquidate the assets of Binningtons and Hull City Motor Works (Kingston Motors), although that relating to the latter was subsequently postponed and the firm continued as a wholly-owned subsidiary for several more years.

According to figures published in 1933, East Yorkshire at that time were operating a total of 145 buses and coaches over 36 routes. The vehicles were allocated to depots at Aldborough (8); Bridlington - Cliff Street (3); Bridlington - Havelock Crescent (30); Driffield (27); Elloughton (13); Goole (4); Anlaby Road, Hull (100); Scarborough (15) and Withernsea (8). The figures shown relate to the accommodation available at each depot and not necessarily the number of vehicles allocated to each. In addition, a further 35 vehicles were owned by the two wholly-owned subsidiaries who between them operated a further 7 routes.Traffic statistics show that in 1930 the number of passengers carried totalled 7,202,456, this rising to 7,361,673 in 1931 and 8,975,567 in 1932 whilst the number of bus miles run in the years 1930-2 were 4,317,792; 4,371,518 and 4,750,254 respectively. In Hull, the registered

office was located at 252 Anlaby Road adjacent to the garage, while the traffic office was at Leyton Chambers, Paragon Street. Additionally, an office was maintained at Piccadilly, York.

During 1933 it was found necessary to find suitable accommodation for a proper booking office at Bridlington to replace the inadequate facilities at Cliff Street and as a result negotiations were set in motion for a garage area on the promenade. Eventually a small garage space was found near Fox's Garage in Princes Street and this was purchased by the company for development as a bus station towards the end of the year.

Throughout the latter months of the year, discussions had been taking place with Hull Corporation in an attempt to reach a co-ordination agreement providing an 'A' area around the city centre from which the Corporation would receive all the revenue from both operators and a 'B' area covering the city's suburbs in which the mileage and receipts would be shared. The territory beyond, designated the 'C' area would be the sole domain of East Yorkshire and an area in which the Corporation would not operate. Eventually, full agreement was reached and although a commencement date of 1 April 1934 was set, in the event a few minor points which required clarification caused this to be postponed until 29 July when the co-ordination finally came into force. From a conductor's point of view, the co-ordination scheme must have been a nightmare, for in 1934 Bell Punch rack-type tickets were being exclusively used by the company. Thus, when working routes which passed through A, B & C areas, conductors were required to carry three different ticket racks, one for each area. Quickly seeing how laborious this previously simple ticketing system had now become, the company began seeking a less complicated replacement system which could be used equally inside and outside the co-ordination zones.

After investigating a number of different fares collection systems, a new method of ticketing was devised by a prominent manufacturer in co-ordination with East Yorkshire in which waybill compilation was speedier and the number of tickets required was greatly reduced. Named the 'Willebrew' system after its inventors, *Will*amson (ticket printers), *Eb*rey (manager of East Yorkshire) and *Brew*er (a director of Williamsons), multifare tickets were used in conjunction with a guillotine maching. The internal blade cut off a portion of the ticket, leaving the the guillotined section which showed all fares in excess of that paid, inside the machine and from these 'off-cuts', the conductors takings were able to be

*Two of the range of Willebrew tickets used by East Yorkshire*

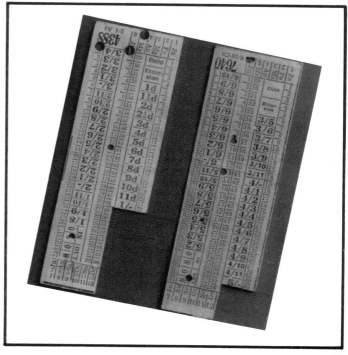

*Fitted with ECOC 28-seat coach bodywork built to BEF design and specification is 263, a 1934 Leyland TS6 caught by the camera at Alfreton, Derbyshire in May 1935 whilst operating a limited stop journey to Birmingham. (G.H.F.Atkins/EYMS)*

calculated by the office staff. Only 7 separate tickets were required to serve all the zones and those for the A & B areas were printed in two-tone colours for ease of recognition. The stage direction and cancellation of return tickets was carried out by the use of hand clippers carried by the conductor and so successful was the Willebrew system, that it continued in use by East Yorkshire for almost 36 years before it was completely superceded by Setright machines.

A total of 34 new buses and coaches joined the fleet in 1934, these including 20 Leyland TS6s of which 11 had bus bodywork by Brush and 9 were coaches, 6 bodied by ECOC and 3 by English Electric. The remaining 14 were Brush highbridge-bodied Leyland TD3s, 10 being of conventional styling and the final four to East Yorkshire's own specification. On the latter, the top deck was tapered slightly inwards and the roof was specially shaped to correspond with the Gothic arch of Beverley Bar, an obstacle built in 1409 under which vehicles had to pass to gain access to Beverley town centre. These buses set the scene as far as East Yorkshire double deckers were concerned for over 30 years. Apart from the special contour of their roof, another unusual feature of these 'Beverley Bar' (and all subsequent) double deckers was the application of a broad white band

around the edge of the roof. This, it was felt, created the optical illusion of a normally-shaped bus and tended to hide the high peak of the roof to some degree. This band, painted along each side of the roof and across the front dome (but for some unknown reason not continued on to the rear dome) was perpetuated until the demise of the blue livery in the 'seventies, and strangely was even applied to low-height buses such as the AEC Renowns and Bristol VRTs. Furthermore it was revived when the Routemasters acquired in 1988 received the traditional livery, officially described as indigo, primrose and white.

In May 1934, plans were passed for the new bus station at Bridlington and a tender of £3,500 was accepted for its construction. At this same time tenders were invited for extensions to Anlaby Common workshops which were to include offices for the clerical staff. Whilst on the subject of premises, mention must be made of the company's purchase in July of 2,000 shares in Blackpool Omnibus Stations Ltd., 1,850 of these going to East Yorkshire Motor Services Ltd., the remaining 150 to W.S.Wreathall. In January 1935, the company purchased a further 300 £1 shares in London Coastal Coaches, a concern in which they already had a

*Left : The first buses to be fitted with Beverley Bar-contoured roofs were four Brush-bodied Leyland TD3s delivered in 1934. One of these, 272 is pictured here when brand new. (EYMS)*

*Below : New in 1934, this Leyland TS6 - 268 - was fitted with English Electric 30-seat coach bodywork for use on the company's long distance Limited Stop services. It is seen here at Huntingdon Street bus station, Nottingham in August 1938 enroute to Scarborough and shows the ornate EYMS logo used on these particular coaches on its side panels. (G.H.F.Atkins/EYMS)*

This 1939 scene in Hull shows Brush-bodied Leyland TD3 245 enroute to Withernsea. New in 1934, this was one of the last double deckers delivered to East Yorkshire with conventionally-shaped roofs, all subsequent orders specifying Beverley Bar-contoured upper decks.

When new in 1929, Leyland TS2 121 was fitted with a Hall Lewis coach body. In 1936 it was downgraded to stage carriage duties and given a new Roe body with which it is seen here some ten years later, a few months before its final withdrawal from service.      (EYMS)

financial investment, and additionally bought a plot of land adjacent to their Bannister Street garage at Withernsea to enable these premises to be extended when required. This need turned out to be sooner rather than later and by November of this same year, the extension had been completed, as had that at Anlaby Common workshops. The new bus station at Bridlington was finished by the scheduled date and was opened at Easter 1935, providing this seaside resort with facilities far better than it had previously enjoyed.

The last major independent operator to be purchased before World War II was Sharpes Motors Ltd. of Hedon, a firm to which approaches had been made as long ago as April 1928. F.Sharpe, a cycle and repairs shop owner in Hedon bought his first bus, a Bracebridge-bodied 14-seat Ford TT in April 1922 when he started a private hire business. Elated by success from this venture, he purchased a second Ford TT chassis for which he built his own body, using his original vehicle as a pattern. Having doubled his fleet, he started a service from Hedon to Hull on 5 July 1922 and during the following year added a Barnaby-bodied Ford-Baico model T; and Albion charabanc; a Daimler CB 20-seater and a Crossley charabanc to his fleet. Although no additional services were opened, Sharpe's private hire business continued to expand and between 1925 and 1930 2 Guy Bs; 3 Guy BBs; a Morris Commercial and an Albion were purchased, some of which replaced older members of the fleet. On 16 July 1935 Sharpe sold his business and 6 vehicles to East Yorkshire, but in view of the fact that EYMS and Hull Corporation now had their co-ordination agreement and that Sharpe's route passed into the city 'A' area, the Corporation claimed a half share in the takeover. After much discussion, this matter was settled in November when the Corporation were successful in gaining an equal share in the Sharpe's business.

On 27 August the territorial agreement with United Automobile Services ended by mutual consent and following the decision taken some eighteen months earlier, the wholly-owned subsidiary Binningtons was liquidated in May and conveyance of the premises at Cliff Road, Hornsea to East Yorkshire was confirmed.

During 1935 a number of older vehicles were sold and to replace them and also increase the size of the fleet 6 Leyland TD4s with Brush 'Beverley Bar' roofed double deckers, 7 Brush bus-bodied Leyland TS7s and 3 English Electric-bodied TS7 coaches were purchased. Additionally, the 2 ex.Hull City Motor Works Leyland PLSC3s were despatched to Chas.H. Roe of Leeds where they were fitted with new 32-seat front entrance bus bodies.

Below : The first bus to be converted for use in East Yorkshire's ancillary fleet was Leyland LB5 YM6649. New to Lee & Beaulah as a double decker in 1926, it was converted into a breakdown wagon in 1935 and remained in use until its final withdrawal in June 1947.   (EYMS)

Below : Acquired with the business of Hull City Motor Works (Kingston) in 1932, 199, a Leyland Lion PLSC3 new in 1928 was given a new Roe body in 1935 which resulted in its continuance in service until 1940. It is seen here in Vine Street depot, Scarborough in June 1935.
(G.H.F.Atkins/EYMS)

*Originally petrol-engined, 1935 Duple coach-bodied Leyland TS7 291, like its two sisters, was fitted with an oil engine in 1937. Seen here at Huntingdon Street bus station, Nottingham in July 1936, this coach was requisitioned by the Ministry of War Transport in October 1941 and never returned to the company.*
*(G.H.F.Atkins/EYMS)*

*Resting at Northway bus station, Scarborough in June 1950 a few months before its withdrawal from service is 286, a 1935 Brush-bodied Leyland TS7.     (G.H.F.Atkins/EYMS)*

*Making its debut in May 1937, Leyland TS7 304 was fitted with coach-seated bodywork built by ECW to BEF specification. It is pictured here at Huntingdon Street bus station, Nottingham in August 1937 while operating the Scarborough to London service.     (G.H.F.Atkins/EYMS)*

The old Lister Street premises in Hull which since June 1929 had been leased to Hull Corporation and others were vacated in January 1935 and later in the year were sold. Meanwhile, more land was acquired at Bridlington in St.John Street near the Old Town and plans were submitted in February 1936 for the construction of a new depot on this site. These were approved and building began in earnest during the summer months, this being completed in October 1937. Still on the property side, a new lease was agreed with Watson & Co. at Goole for the garage in Bridge Street which had been rented by East Yorkshire since 1929.

Three new Duple bodied 28-seat front entrance Leyland TS7 joined the fleet in 1936 as did 11 Brush-bodied Leyland TD4 double deckers with the now familiar 'Beverly Bar' style of bodywork. The final four of the TD4s were fitted with torque converters and carried the legend 'Gearless Bus' on their radiator grilles. In addition to the arrival of these new vehicles, the fleet was further updated by the rebodying of 6 of the 1929 Leyland TS2 coaches with new Roe 30-seat bus bodywork and one of the 1932 ex.Binnington TD2s hich was given a new Brush body complete with 'Beverley Bar' style roof.

*Amongst the Leyland TS8s purchased in 1938 were five fitted with Roe dual-purpose bodies built to BEF specification. The side flash enhanced the appearance of these vehicles which were regularly used on the company's long Limited Stop services. Here 345 rests at Huntingdon Street bus station, Nottingham in August 1938 whilst enroute from Hull to London. Details of the route are carried on boards mounted above the side windows.*
*(G.H.F.Atkins/EYMS)*

On 3 May 1936 the first strike of any consequence took place, but happily this was quickly resolved and four days later, their honour having been satisfied, the staff returned to work. Later in the year East Yorkshire and Hull Corporation both agreed to carry blind persons free of charge within the A & B areas for an experimental period and this was implemented on 1 December and continued until 28 July 1938.

All the 1937 intake of new vehicles were single deckers based on Leyland TS7 chassis. 6 had ECW 28-seat rear entrance coach bodies, 6 had ECW 32-seat rear entrance dual purpose bodies and the remaining 12 were equipped with 30-seat rear entrance bus bodywork. The latter sported an oval-shaped window in their rear bulkhead, a traditional feature of East Yorkshire's single deck buses for many years. During 1937, 14 of the company's Leyland double deckers had their petrol engines replaced by new 8.6 litre oil engines in order to improve their fuel economy.

Due to the lack of terminal accommodation in the centre of Hull, the company arranged with the Corporation to use three platforms in the municipal bus station in Ferensway at a cost of £1,800 per year and thus from 16 June, East Yorkshire were able to terminate all their Hull services at one central point. This bus station had been opened by the Corporation on 22 October 1935.

After the comparative calm of the previous couple of years, 1938 proved to be more eventful and on 25 January the directors reported that the liquidation of the wholly-owned subsidiary Hull City Motor Works had commenced. As the lease held jointly with West Yorkshire Road Car Co.Ltd. for the garage at Vine Street, Scarborough was due to expire later in the year, a decision as to whether to take up the purchase option or seek another site had to be taken and it was the latter course that was to be followed. In July, a site was found in Northway, not far from the railway station and town centre and after joint discussions, it was decided to submit plans to Scarborough Corporation for the erection of a garage. Consent was given and the land was duly purchased in January 1939, albeit by West Yorkshire and while construction work was in progress, the road in Northway was used as a temporary terminus. Meanwhile, at Driffield extensions to the garage were built in July 1938, thus increasing its capacity and improving its facilities.

Returning to the fleet, a massive total of 46 new vehicles made their debut during 1938, 25 of which were Leyland TD5s with highbridge 'Beverley Bar' style bodies by Brush (15) and ECW (10). The single deckers were all Leyland TS8s, 15 of them having ECW B32R bodywork, 5 with Roe DP28R bodies and 1 with Roe B32R coachwork. Following a decision in March to withdraw and sell the 10 Leyland TD1s of 1929 vintage, most of which had had their open rear stairs enclosed some years earlier, a change of policy resulted in 10 new ECW bodies being ordered in May at a cost of £787.2.0d each for fitting to the TD1 chassis in order to prolong their lives in East Yorkshire. In November however, after giving this matter further consideration, it was agreed to sell 7 of these buses and to convert the remaining 3 to open top configuration for use on the Bridlington to Flamborough summer services. The order with ECW was not cancelled however but was increased to 11 for fitting to newly-ordered Leyland TD5 chassis. These buses entered service in November 1939 and were followed in December by 8 Leyland TS8s with ECW 30-seat rear entrance bus bodywork. The 3 Leyland TD1s converted to open top during the winter of 1938/9 entered service at Bridlington at the start of the summer 1939 season and immediately proved popular, particularly with holiday makers and it is a pity that these buses were not used again in this capacity after the end of the summer.

At Hull, the co-ordination agreement with the Corporation was renewed for a further five years on 1 January 1939 while a few months later, East Yorkshire purchased a further 200 £1 shares in London Coastal Coaches.

One of the three 1929 Leyland-bodied TD1s converted to open-top configuration in 1938 for use at Bridlington, open-staircase 132 along with its sisters was withdrawn from service after operating only two summer seasons in their new form. It is seen here carrying posters publicising the service upon which it was operated.

370, one of ten ECW-bodied Leyland TD5s purchased in 1938 is seen here at Scarborough in June 1950. Sporting Beverley Bar-shaped roofs, these buses also employed an unusual three-window layout to their front upper deck bulkhead - a style favoured by East Yorkshire in pre-war years. (G.H.F.Atkins/EYMS)

# THE INTERVENTION OF WAR

War was declared on 3 September 1939 and almost immediately its first effects were experienced. Blackout regulations were introduced and in an attempt to economise on fuel, numerous services were cut or reduced in frequency and express and long distance routes were suspended completely. As a result of these cuts, a number of buses and coaches were delicensed and many of these never saw further service with East Yorkshire.

A scheme to cover company losses as a result of enemy action was entered into by insurances through the British Electric Federation which gave additional cover to East Yorkshire from October 1939 and plans were approved to provide air raid shelters at Anlaby Common workshops and

January 1940 purchased a further 100 £1 shares in London Coastal Coaches and 150 shares in Blackpool Omnibus Stations Ltd. In addition, they made a loan of £1,200 to the latter company and during the following month purchased the Newcastle to Hull licence of George Galley (Galley's Express Motors) of Newcastle upon Tyne for £2,000 despite being unable to operate this service at that time. In March 1940 authorisation was given for the installation of three 10,000 gallon fuel tanks at Anlaby Road depot, but in the event only two were fitted. Finally, in October the Military Authorities took over the company's Hull Road depot at Anlaby.

1941 saw the loan of further buses to the RAF at Catfoss with 1 TS1 going in January and 2 more of the same type in

*Left : The last buses delivered to pre-war specification were a trio of Weymann-bodied Leyland TS8s built to BEF design which made their debut in the autumn of 1940. The last of these, 395 is seen here at Hull in 1953.*

*Below : One of a pair of unfrozen Leyland TD7s purchased in 1942, 397 seen here is fitted with a Brush body of wartime specification which featured a Beverley bar-contoured roof.*

Elloughton, Bridlington and Driffield depots at a total cost of £700.

Towards the end of the year, the company's Hallgate premises at Cottingham were taken over by the Military Authorities and in December an impressment order was made in respect of 3 of the 1935 Brush-bodied Leyland TS7s. One of these was collected immediately, the other 2 following in February 1940 together with one of the company's 1-ton Morris Commercial lorries. As replacements for these, East Yorkshire were authorised to order 3 6-cylinder engined single deckers which in September 1940 materialised as Leyland TS8s fitted with British Electrical Federation-style 30-seat rear entrance bus bodies by Weymann. These proved to be the last pre-war buses received by the company for although 24 Weymann-bodied Leyland TS11 single deckers and 14 Leyland TD7 double deckers had been ordered, due to the escalation of the war, none of these were built.

Further vehicles to leave the fleet were 8 Leyland Lion PLSC3s which were requisitioned by the Ministry of Supply in May/June 1940 and 8 PLSC3s which in June were loaned to the South Staffordshire Regiment at Welton, Yorkshire. The latter were also impressed by the Ministry of War Transport in August and none of these ever returned to their rightful owner. In October, Crosville Motor Services who suddenly found themselves in need of a large number of additional buses for use on services to Ordnance factories, approached East Yorkshire for help. This resulted in 24 buses being immediately sent on extended loan (6 PLSC3s; 9 TS2s; 5 LT1s and 4 TS4s). Before the year ended, a further 2 Leyland TS2s left the fleet, these being loaned to the RAF at Catfoss where they were used for the transportation of personnel to satellite airfields.

Despite the nation being locked in war, the company still never missed an opportunity to expand their interests and in

April. These were not away for long however and were returned to the company together with the 2 LT2s in the summer of 1941. In October however, the 3 Duple-bodied Leyland TS7 coaches of 1936 vintage were commandeered by the Ministry of War Transport and, despite being less than 6 years old, this trio were never returned.

Disaster struck in May 1941 when during an enemy air attack on Hull, the company's offices in Leyton Chambers were destroyed along with most of the company's records etc. In urgent need of new accommodation, five rooms were rented at Ferensway House, Paragon Square and these were occupied by early June. Prior to this, on 1 March the new depot and bus station at Northway, Scarborough was opened by West Yorkshire Road Car Co.Ltd. who leased accommodation and facilities to East Yorkshire for their joint use. The final development of the year came in October when some land and buildings next to 252 Anlaby Road, Hull were purchased for future use.

A change in control took place in 1942 when B.E.T. and Tilling divided their interests and the T.B.A.T. was wound up. As a result, T.B.A.T's shareholding in East Yorkshire passed to a new company named B.E.T.Omnibus Services Ltd.

In an attempt to overcome the general shortage of buses at that time experienced by many operators throughout Britain, the Government authorised the completion of chassis already under construction when bus manufacturing ceased or for which manufacturers had components in stock. Generally referred to as 'unfrozen' buses, these were allocated to operators by the Ministry of Supply and two such buses were directed to East Yorkshire. Leyland TD7s with Brush bodywork built to MoS specification and numbered 396/7 by the company, these arrived in September 1942 and were immediately placed in service as valuable additions to the fleet. Before their arrival, the company had submitted an application to the MoS for up to 40 petrol engined Bedford OWB single deckers and although this was at first granted, the authorisation was withdrawn in December and thus no vehicles of this type ever entered the fleet. Instead, between October 1942 and January 1944 the Ministry issued licences to the company for the delivery of 22 Guy Arab double deckers, of which more later.

By the autumn of 1942, following experiments carried out elsewhere in the country with producer gas propulsion, East Yorkshire were directed to join the Government's scheme and adapt a number of vehicles to this type of fuel and in October the Minister of War Transport stated that he expected 17 conversions by July 1943. The estimated cost of this was £3,000 and in the event only 12 buses were so converted, these all being Leylands and comprising 1 TD1; 7 TD3s; 2 TS2s and 2 TS6s. In March 1943, 12 of the buses loaned to Crosville were returned and placed in store and of these, only 3 saw further service with East Yorkshire, the remainder being sold soon after the end of the war.

Despite the intensive bombing suffered by Hull during the dark years of World War II, surprisingly few of East Yorkshire's vehicles were damaged as a result of these air attacks, although in order to minimise risks, the company asked Hull Corporation to allow vehicles to be dispersed on roads in West Park (about half a mile from Anlaby Road depot) and to an area around the Boulevard. To this the Corporation readily agreed and thus after their last runs each night, buses were driven to these points by depot shunters, many of whom were members of East Yorkshire Motor Services Home Guard platoon. The Home Guard stayed on duty all night, returning the buses to Anlaby Road depot in time to take up their duties on the following morning. It soon became a common sight to see lines of buses standing in the park or round the Boulevard, but this undoubtedly led to greater safety for the fleet. A mobile canteen was set up on spare ground owned by the LNER in Collier Street, Hull.

During December 1943 the company sold their Walton Street premises to N.W.Transport Services Ltd for £3,950, this building having been surplus to requirements as a result of the extensions added to Anlaby Road depot. Prior to this, in February 1943, the first of the wartime Guy double deckers were received, these being Arab Is with Gardner 5LW engines and Brush highbridge bodies built to MoS specifications. 3 of these buses were placed in service immediately with a further 2 following in July. 5 more Brush bodied Guys - this time Gardner 5LW-engined Arab IIs - arrived between May and October 1944 and these were joined in November/December by 10 Arab IIs with Roe highbridge bodies, all of which were built to MoS specification. Like the earlier wartime Arabs, these had 'Beverley Bar' contoured roofs, one of the very few permitted variations to the national 'utility' standard body design. Coinciding with their arrival was the return of 6 more single deckers from Crosville, these terminating their loan during the penultimate month of the year. An unfortunate incident in October resulted in one of the 1934 Brush-bodied Leyland TD3s being severely damaged by fire. After overhauling the chassis, this was then despatched to Willowbrook at Loughborough where in November it was fitted with a new 51-seat lowbridge body to MoS specification at a cost of £1,200.

By now, the restraints of war were easing slightly and the producer gas buses - which had never proved popular with either crews or passengers - were able to be re-converted to operate on more conventional fuels. The producer gas trailers, which had become a familiar sight being towed behind the vehicles concerned, were then placed in store as insurance should the situation worsen again.

The opening month of 1945 saw the arrival of another 2 Roe highbridge-bodied Guy Arab IIs and surprisingly these were licensed for service immediately despite the 8 delivered in November 1944 still remaining in store and having yet to see active service with East Yorkshire. These subsequently

*Resting between duties at Scarborough in June 1950 is 402, a wartime Guy Arab I with Brush bodywork incorporating a Beverley Bar-shaped roof. This bus was given a new body by Roe in 1953 and remained in service until 1961. (G.H.F.Atkins/EYMS)*

were progressively licensed throughout 1945 with the last taking up its duties in August.

During 1945, 8 Leyland TS8 single deckers and 7 TD5 double deckers were fitted for snowplough duties and remained so equipped until the early 1950s. Although the fitments were retained throughout this period, these buses were not confined to these duties and were operated normally in service for most of the time.

Surprisingly, almost all of East Yorkshire's fleet retained its familiar dark blue & primrose livery throughout the war years and despite the company's geographical location in the proximity of the port of Hull and close to several military airfields, few of its vehicles succumbed to the khaki livery applied by numerous other operators in various parts of Britain during that period of time.

# RETURN TO PEACE

With the war now having ended, plans were quickly drawn up for fleet replacements and operational expansion and in July 1945 orders were placed for 9 new double deckers and 14 saloons for delivery as soon as possible. A large number of obsolete buses which had been in store for much of the war were released for sale and no fewer than 20 of these (6 Leyland PLSC3s, 12 TD1s and 2 TD2s) were disposed of to a dealer in Brixton, London who, early in 1946 despatched these to Holland as part of the U.N.R.R.A. scheme.

Early in 1946, services began to run normally again and to meet the demand for additional vehicles, a number of coaches and buses which had been delicensed for two or more years were returned to service in April. Orders were placed during this same month for a further 20 double deckers and 8 single deckers, these being in addition to the 3 coaches ordered in February. For reasons unknown, the latter were cancelled in June 1947.

A plot of land at Northgate, Cottingham was sold by the company in the early part of the year whilst in June, East Yorkshire made a 'double-edged' offer to George Crosby of Hunmanby for the purchase of his business. Whilst the company made a joint offer with United Automobile Services, they also bid £4,100 on their own account, thus trying to get two bites of the cherry. No response was made to either offer however, and so East Yorkshire increased their offer to a ceiling of £7,000.

In September, the Military Authorities offered back to the company for £1,500 one of the 1936 Duple-bodied Leyland TS7 coaches it had requisitioned in 1941. Although this was re-purchased, it was never placed back in service and instead was sold during the following month to an operator in Lancashire. The rented property at Aldborough was purchased from the lessor in November 1946 for the sum of £1,625, the garage then being retained whilst the frontage was re-sold. In June of the following year, the old Springville Motor Services garage in Hull Road, Hessle was sold for £2,100 following its use by the Military Authorities during the war. The most notable occurrence of 1947 however was the arrival of the first new buses since the war, these making their debut in January. Deliveries continued throughout the year and by December no fewer than 34 had been received. Of these, 26 were Leyland PD1s with Roe highbridge bodywork incorporating Beverley Bar-style roofs; 2 were Leyland PD1s with Roe lowbridge bodies and the remaining 5 were Leyland PS1s fitted with Weymann 30-seat rear entrance bus bodywork. During this same year, the ECW body fitted to 1939 Leyland TD5 379 was rebuilt by Northern Motor Utilities of York.

Towards the end of 1946, Sheffield Corporation had found themselves acutely short of servicable buses and whilst approaching operators throughout the North and Midlands for help, asked East Yorkshire if they could hire any of their

*Right : The first post-war buses to enter service with East Yorkshire were Roe-bodied Leyland PD1s which made their debut in January 1947. 420, seen here at Hull typified this batch with its painted radiator shell and Beverley Bar shaped roof.*

*Below : The first single deckers to join the East Yorkshire fleet after the war had ended were five Weymann-bodied Leyland PS1s, one of which - 430 - is seen here at Pocklington in the mid 1950s.*

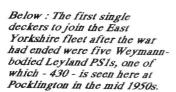

*Above : The first post war addition to East Yorkshire's ancillary fleet was Morris Commercial CV11/40 lorry HAT422 which was used mainly to carry spares and sundry items between the company's depots. (EYMS)*

vehicles. Although themselves awaiting new buses and thus having few surplus at that time, the company was able to offer 3 single deckers and these were gratefully accepted. The buses concerned were the 3 Leyland-bodied TS2s acquired from Binningtons which had previously been on loan to Crosville during the early part of the war. Upon their return from Chester, they had been placed in store until July 1946 when they were re-licensed for occasional use. Thus, in January 1947 this trio departed for Sheffield where they gave yeoman service until their return in May.

Upon the nationalisation of the railway companies in 1947, the LNER share in East Yorkshire passed to the British Transport Commission.

Although at first no response was received from George Crosby in respect of any of the offers made to him for his business during the previous year, in the autumn of 1947 he suddenly intimated that he would accept £6,500 and an agreement was reached for the transfer of his services etc. to East Yorkshire on 1 November. George Crosby, who had a garage in Stonegate, Hunmanby near Filey had decided in May 1923 to run a bus service from his home village to Scarborough and for this purpose purchased a 17-seat Atlas which he painted in a red & white livery and operated under the fleet name 'Red & White Bus Co.'. Almost immediately, a second service was opened from Hull to Newport, but as this did not come up to his expectations it was soon discontinued. In February 1926, a 20-seat Thornycroft demonstrator was

purchased and this was followed in June by a 14-seat Chevrolet. In addition to his Scarborough service, Crosby also began to develop private hire work and in 1930 added another Thornycroft A1 and a pair of BAT single deckers (all secondhand) to his fleet. During the years which followed, he opened two variations to his route, one serving Cayton Bay, the other, Seamer, and between 1933 and 1938 purchased 4 Bedford coaches, by which time his fleet name had been changed to 'Crosby's Bus Service'. After the war, another Bedford was bought, this being a Duple 30-seat bus bodied OB which arrived in September 1946. In addition to operating from his garage at Stonegate, Hunmanby, he also rented a garage in the village at Northgate and in the late 'twenties/ early 'thirties he additionally operated from The County Garage, St.Thomas Street, Scarborough. Although 5 of his Bedfords passed to East Yorkshire along with his services on 1 November 1947, none of these vehicles were used by their new owner and were stored at Cliff Street depot, Bridlington before being sold in December. Crosby's premises were not included in the deal and he continued to trade as a motor repairer and car dealer after 1947.

In March 1948, more new buses began to arrive and by July, 17 Brush-bodied 30-seat rear entrance buses and 3 ECW bodied 31-seat dual purpose vehicles had been placed in service, all on Leyland PS1 chassis. Although no new double deckers were received during this year, 15 of the 1938/9 Leyland TD5s were given new highbridge 'Beverley Bar' bodies by ECW. Additionally, in April 1948 the Chairman

notified the directors of his intention to purchase 3 coaches from Sheffield United Tours for £8,621.3.6d and that he had agreed that East Yorkshire should sell 3 dual purpose vehicles to Sheffield United at an agreed price before 31 March 1949. Whilst the three ex.SUT coaches - 1947 AEC Regals with Duple 33-seat bodies - arrived in May, in the event no dual purpose vehicles were sold in exchange. Entering service in June 1948, the three acquired coaches at first retained their former owner's red & grey livery but were adorned with East Yorkshire fleet names.

The 5 rooms rented at Ferensway House, Paragon Square, Hull were vacated during 1948 when the staff moved to the offices located in Anlaby Road, and in the early summer, a new bus station was opened in Filey, this being shared with United. Finally, in September the company applied for compensation in respect of 18 buses requisitioned by Government Departments during the war which were not returned. The sum claimed was £5,132.10.0d plus 2% interest from the date of acquisition.

All except one of the 1939 Leyland TD5s were given new ECW bodies in 1948. Although built largely to standard ECW Tilling Group specification, they were fitted with Beverley Bar-style roofs as illustrated by 383 at Hull in 1955, a year before it was withdrawn from service.

537, a 1950 Roe-bodied 8ft. wide Leyland PD2/3 shows the inward-angled upper deck windows and specially-shaped roof necessary to allow it to safely pass beneath the Gothic arch at Beverley. It is seen here leaving Hull on a journey to Willerby Square in 1964.

38 new Leyland PD1A double deckers made their debut in 1949, 35 of which had Roe 'Beverley Bar'-type 54-seat highbridge bodies, the remaining three having 51-seat lowbridge bodies by this same coachbuilder. In November the leases of both the Bridge Street garage at Goole and the Cliff Street premises at Bridlington expired and neither were renewed whilst early the following year a temporary booking office was opened in Hull at Collier Street, adjacent to Ferensway bus station. This was closed towards the end of 1950 when a permanent booking and enquiry office was opened in the bus station itself.

Another large intake of new vehicles was received in 1950 when 5 Leyland PD1As and 24 Leyland PD2/3s took up their duties. All were fitted with Roe highbridge bodies featuring 'Beverley Bar'-contoured roofs and the PD2/3s were the first 8ft. wide vehicles in the fleet. Joining these were 7 Burlingham-bodied 33-seat Leyland PS2/3 luxury coaches which, although delivered in August/December 1949 were not placed in service until the beginning of the 1950 summer season.

During 1950, East Yorkshire began to look at their livery which had not changed since the formation of the company in 1926. Although not dissatisfied with their indigo blue & primrose, they nevertheless decided to experiment with new colour schemes and to test public reaction with these. As a result of their deliberations, wartime Guy Arab 402 was

painted in a medium blue & cream while 509, a Roe-bodied Leyland PD1A was repainted purple & primrose. The comments received from the public relating to these experiments were far from favourable and it was not long before both buses had reverted to their original colours which were to be retained until the early 'seventies.

At the start of 1951, an approach was made to R.Williamson & Sons of Bridlington for the purchase of their two stage carriage licences within that town. These licences quickly became the subject of discussion between Williamsons, East Yorkshire, the Traffic Commissioners and John Boddy of Boddy's Motors who had an agreement with Williamson relating to these particular services and had already started to prepare his company for their eventual takeover. After giving this saga due consideration, the Traffic Commissioner ruled that the B.E.T. company should operate Williamson's licences and as a result, Boddy was compensated and East Yorkshire took over the operations on 1 February.

John Williamson had started up in business as long ago as 1885 as a jobmaster, hiring out horse-drawn wagonettes abd charabancs from Hilderthorpe Road Mews. His sons, Robert, Reuben and Charles at first all gave a hand with the

525, a Burlingham-bodied Leyland PS2/3 coach was one of seven delivered in 1949, all of which were then stored until the spring of 1950 before entering service. Originally built as 28-seaters for use on the company's extended tours, they were re-seated to accommodate 32 passengers in 1952 and remained in service for a further nine years.

*East Yorkshire's first underfloor-engined buses made their debut in 1951 in the form of seven Brush-bodied Leyland Royal Tiger PSU1/13s. One of these, 552, is seen here enroute to Selby during the mid 'fifties.*

*The only Leyland-bodied double deckers purchased by East Yorkshire in post-war years were six lowbridge PD2/12s which made their debut in 1951. One of these buses, 588 rests at Hull alongside Park Royal-bodied AEC Bridgemaster 752 in 1966.*

business, although Charles later became a fellmonger in the Beeford area, leaving his two brothers to continue. Following Reuben's retirement, his sons Charles and Walter (known as Tim) decided to operate a proper bus service from Bridlington Quay to the Market Place in the Old Town and from their premises at Havelock Crescent, this commencing in the early 1890s. Later, in 1907, an open-top Herald Motor Co. double deck motor bus was purchased for use on this route, and this continued in service until 1920 when it was replaced by a more modern Republic fitted with a 1912 former horse-bus open-top body. Due to its temperemental nature, the Republic only saw spasmodic use and as a result, the service frequently had to revert to horse-drawn vehicles.

A second service was introduced, this plying along Bridlington's sea front, but due to numerous problems arising from Trown & Tooth who also operated over part of this route undercutting fares, this was soon withdrawn. 3 more double deckers were purchased between 1920 and 1922, these being a Tilling Stevens TTA1 petrol electric, a Y-type Daimler and a Leyland and following these came a variety of Daimler, Morris Commercial, Ford and Gilford single deckers to bring the fleet total to around 10 vehicles by the outbreak of World War II. Between 1 November 1923 and 31 October 1926, Williamsons had carried 2,041,228 passengers and had only three complaints recorded against them.

*Below : Purchased in 1947, this former military Chevrolet was used by East Yorkshire's Engineering Department both as a towing wagon and for tree pruning duties until December 1956.*

*In a similar manner to several other BET companies, East Yorkshire purchased a number of Beadle chassisless coaches during 1951/2 which used the mechanical units removed from pre-war double deckers. 559, which made its debut in 1951 incorporated units removed from the company's 1936 Leyland TD4 300. (EYMS)*

*One of the Weymann-bodied Leyland Royal Tiger buses purchased by East Yorkshire in 1952, 603 originally sported a rear entrance but was rebuilt to front entrance layout by Roe in 1959 to make it suitable for one-person-operation. It is seen here in its latter form at Beverley in 1965.*

*After giving only a couple of years service, the coach-bodied Leyland PD2/12s were all down-graded to normal bus status and repainted into East Yorkshire's standard dark blue & primrose livery. 577 is seen here in its new guise leaving Hull at the start of its journey to Withernsea in 1964.*

During the 1939-45 war, several secondhand Leyland single deckers were purchased but it was not until 1947 that double deckers once again appeared in the Williamson fleet. These comprised 2 Cowieson-bodied Leyland TD1s acquired from Glasgow Corporation and a pair of Roe centre-entrance TD2s originating from Yorkshire Woollen District Transport. These were joined in 1948 by three more Yorkshire W.D. centre-entrance TD2s and in 1949 by a pair of three-axle buses (a Leyland TT5c and an AEC Renown) from Doncaster Corporation. Although Williamson's two licences and eight vehicles - all in Williamson's white & blue livery - passed to East Yorkshire on 1 February 1951 for £11,500, due to their antiquity none of the vehicles were operated by their new owner and indeed it was left to Williamson to dispose of them.

Returning to East Yorkshire's own fleet, 1951 saw the arrival of their first underfloor-engined single deckers, 7 Brush-bodied 44-seat rear entrance Leyland PSU1/13 Royal Tigers, and the company's first chassisless vehicles. These had been built by J.C.Beadle of Dartford who used the mechanical components from two of East Yorkshire's 1936 Leyland TD4 double deckers to produce a pair of 35-seat single deck coaches which were destined to give nine years service. Completing the 1951 intake of new buses were 6 all-Leyland PD2/12s with lowbridge bodywork. 2 Leyland PD1s and 6 PS1s were fitted with snowplough equipment to replace earlier similarly-modified vehicles which had now been withdrawn.

Another 8 chassisless Beadle single deckers were delivered early in 1952, these being built from units removed from the company's 1935-7 Leyland TD4s, and were joined by a further 16 underfloor-engined Royal Tigers, this time

with 42-seat rear entrance bus bodywork by Weymann. The most striking vehicles to arrive in 1952 however were 16 Leyland PD2/12s fitted with full-fronted 50-seat coach bodies by Chas.H. Roe. Purchased for use on the company's longer services, these were fitted with rear platform doors and incorporated 'Beverley Bar'-contoured roofs. Painted in a predominantly primrose livery with mid-blue trim, they soon gained the nickname 'Yellow Perils'. Their lives were comparatively short in their original form however and in 1954/5 all were downgraded to bus status and were re-seated to accommodate 54 passengers.

After the previous year's deliveries, the new vehicles arriving in 1953 seemed far more ordinary. 7 Roe highbridge 'Beverley Bar'-bodied Leyland PD2/12s arrived in May/June whilst for the coach fleet, 3 Leyland PSU1/15s were purchased, these having 35-seat rear entrance Windover bodies. These were named 'Kingston Star; Bridlington Star' and 'Beverley Star', thus reviving a custom popular in the 1920s when numerous independently owned coaches and charabancs carried exotic names. The wartime Guy Arabs which had given yeoman service for ten or so years were now found to be in poor condition bodily (although their chassis were still very sound) and in order to prolong their lives, it was decided to replace their old bodies with new ones. All 22 of the Guys were so treated and returned to service with their new Roe highbridge bodies between March 1953 and January 1954.

As a result of the intake of new vehicles, the company now found they had slightly more buses than were required to

East Yorkshire purchased a trio of Windover-bodied Leyland Royal Tiger coaches in 1953, one of which - 615 - is seen here on a private hire duty to a 'Milk Cup' football match in the mid 'sixties.

maintain their full schedules and in December 1953 they were able to loan two of their ECW-rebodied pre-war Leyland TD5s to Yorkshire Woollen District Transport of Dewsbury who at that time were experiencing an acute shortage of buses. These returned to Hull - and their more usual duties - in February 1954. In December of that year, the 2 Brush-bodied Leyland TD7s of 1942 vintage also made the journey to Dewsbury to join Yorkshire W.D. on loan and after staying in their new adopted home for just over a year, both were sold by Yorkshire on East Yorkshire's behalf without returning to Hull.

Further consoildation was achieved on 12 November 1953 when the business of Everingham Bros. at Pocklington was acquired by East Yorkshire. This well-established operator provided the company with the expansion they had long desired in this area and gave them an additional 16 vehicles. Sidney and Irwin Everingham had been in business in Pocklington as tailors, cycle and motor repairers since around 1904 but it was not until after they had completed their military service in World War I that they decided to enter the field of bus operation. Their first vehicle, an AEC Y-type charabanc, was purchased in February 1920 and was employed on a once-weekly market day service from Pocklington to York. At weekends it was used for private hire duties whilst for the remainder of the time it was fitted with a wagon body and used for the carriage of goods. Later in that year, 2 similar dual-purpose vehicles were purchased (both AECs) and in 1921 the brothers planned three different routes to York, each of which would operate on a twice-weekly basis. Having now outgrown the barn at Red House which they rented for their 'fleet', they erected a new garage in Railway Street where they could house and maintain their vehicles. A local joiner, Bob Manners, was contracted to build an enclosed saloon body for fitting to one of the AEC chassis and it was with this bus that the new routes to York were inaugurated in October 1922. By 1925, due to their popularity, the three services had all begun to be operated daily and during 1925 a fourth service was added, this

serving Melbourne and Elvington enroute to York. In this period the fleet had been expanded by the acquisition of a Bellsize, a Garford, a Daimler and a single deck AEC B-type.

When the Derwent Valley Light Railway was closed to passenger traffic in 1926, the two Everingham brothers were quick to take advantage of the situation and increased the frequency of their services accordingly. Two years later, services were started to Bridlington, Malton, Stamford Bridge and Howden and a schools contract was obtained to serve the villages around Pocklington. The growth of their operating network brought the need for more buses and a number of Thornycrofts were bought together with a Dennis E-type, a Maudslay ML4, a pair of Ford AAs, a 4-ton Leyland amd 2 Leyland PLSCs which were later fitted with diesel engines. Always having an eye for business, Everingham Bros. also set up a parcels agency and before long had some 38 or so agents in a similar number of villages.

In the years leading up to World War II, the fleet was modernised by the replacement of older stock with AEC Regals, Albions, Bedfords, Commers, a Maudslay ML6, a Thornycroft A14, a Dodge RBF and a Leyland Cub, all of which were purchased new.

Soon after the outbreak of war, the company found themselves in the transportation of personnel from Pocklington railway station to the numerous airfields which were under construction in the surrounding area and as the war progressed, so this work was developed further by the carriage of RAF personnel to satellite airfields. Having received a new Barnaby-bodied Leyland TS8 in August 1940, the fleet was further supplemented on 19 August 1942 by the arrival of the company's first double decker, a Leyland TD7 with NCME lowbridge bodywork. During this period of hostilities, 4 more double deckers were obtained, one being a Daimler CWG5 the others being Daimler CWA6s, but unlike the TD7, these all carried highbridge bodywork (1 Massey, 1 NCME and 2 Duple) built to MoS specification. In

Seen when new in 1950, Everingham Bros. Barnaby-bodied AEC Regal III HWF658 passed to East Yorkshire with Everingham's business in November 1953. Given fleet number 658 by its new owner, it remained in service until 1962.

*Seen at Pocklington whilst working a journey to Bridlington a few months before being taken over by East Yorkshire is Everingham Bros. 1944 NCME-bodied Daimler CWA6 DBT152.*

*Pictured at Pocklington in 1955 wearing full East Yorkshire livery are two double deckers acquired two years earlier with the business of Everingham Bros. On the left, 663 is a Daimler CWG5 of 1943 vintage which carries Barnaby bodywork dating from 1950 whilst on the right is 653, a 1945 Duple-bodied Daimler CWA6.*

addition, 3 Bedford OWB single deckers were taken into the fleet between December 1942 and July 1944.

Before the war, Everingham's livery had been cream with a dark blue band, but during the 1939-45 period this was changed to grey with steel blue bands, a colour scheme which was to be retained to the end of the company's operations.

Sadly, Sidney Everingham died on 25 August 1945, leaving his brother Irwin to carry on running the business. As soon as new vehicles became available, a start was made on improving the fleet and in 1947 a pair of AEC Regal buses were purchased, these being joined in 1949/50 by 4 AEC Regal IIIs and a highbridge-bodied AEC Regent III. All except one of the Regal IIIs had bodywork built by Barnaby, the odd one out carrying Harrington bus bodywork, this having been a cancelled order by West Bridgford UDC. Rather than buy further new double deckers, in 1951 it was decided to fit new Barnaby highbridge bodies to two of the wartime Daimlers and in December 1952 both buses returned to service in their new form. The last new vehicles to be purchased comprised a pair of Barnaby-bodied AEC Regal IV underfloor-engined coaches which took up their duties in September 1952. The only secondhand vehicles purchased since 1926 were a former Halifax Corporation English Electric-bodied AEC Regent double decker in 1948 and a pair of Commer Commando coaches acquired in 1952.

When Everingham Bros. was taken over by East Yorkshire in November 1953 for £29,000, they were operating a fleet of 31 vehicles, held a wide range of licences and had garages at Red House, Railway Street and Flacks Yard, Pocklington. Of the 31 vehicles, 15 were withdrawn by East Yorkshire before the end of the year and were sold to a dealer in January 1954. At first, all three of Everingham's former garages were used by their new owner, but as will be seen later, these were ultimately replaced by a single depot within the town. Also inherited from Everingham was a small enquiry office in Pocklington and this was retained by East Yorkshire.

Prior to their major acquisition of 1953, East Yorkshire had been searching Scarborough for a site on which they could open a new bus station, this being brought about by the fact that their agreement with West Yorkshire Road Car Co.Ltd. giving them use of the latter's bus station in Northway was due to expire in December. A site was eventually found at Westwood, behind the railway station, and after successfully negotiating with its owners (British Transport Commission), plans were drawn up and submitted to Scarborough Corporation. These were approved and work began with all

*All East Yorkshire's wartime Guy Arabs were fitted with new Roe bodies during the 1950s in order to extend their lives. One such bus, 1944 Arab II gained its new body in 1953 and is seen here operating a Hull local service some six years later.*

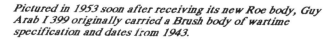

*Pictured in 1953 soon after receiving its new Roe body, Guy Arab I 399 originally carried a Brush body of wartime specification and dates from 1943.*

*One of the 8ft. wide Roe-bodied Leyland PD2/12 double deckers delivered in 1953, 609 shows the way in which the upper deck windows were angled inwards below the specially-shaped roof to enable passage beneath the Gothic arch of Beverley Bar.*

speed, but as the new bus station was not completed by the end of the year, agreement was reached with West Yorkshire allowing them to continue their use of Northway until April 1954. The new bus station at Westwood was opened on 1 May of that year and all East Yorkshire's operations were then transferred to their new site.

Further land was purchased from the British Transport Commission at Railway Street, Pocklington (1050 sq.yds.) to enable a new garage to be built and on 1 May 1954 in addition to opening their new bus station at Scarborough, East Yorkshire also opened a new depot at Cliff Road, Hornsea, this replacing the old Binningtons depot which was sold in December of that year for £7.700. In York, a new

*The last vehicles purchased by Everingham Bros. of Pocklington before their take-over by East Yorkshire in 1953 were a pair of centre-entrance Barnaby-bodied AEC Regal IV coaches, one of which - 662 - is seen here after being repainted into its new owner's colours. (EYMS)*

*The only new vehicles taken into stock during 1954 comprised fourteen Willowbrook dual-purpose-bodied Leyland Tiger Cubs. One of these vehicles, 628 is seen here wearing its predominantly primrose livery operating a private hire duty.*

inspectors' kiosk was opened at 47 Piccadilly, this replacing the kiosk nearby which had been opened in 1935.

On 31 December 1954, E.J.Lee, last of the original 1926 Board members, retired as Resident Director of East Yorkshire Motor Services Ltd, thus severing a link which had existed since the formation of the company some 28 years earlier.

The only new vehicles to join the fleet in 1954 were 14 Leyland PSUC1/2-type Tiger Cubs with 41-seat rear-entrance dual purpose bodywork by Willowbrook. In a primrose livery with mid-blue relief, these took over the company's long distance operations and became regular performers on the London service depite not being equipped to luxury coach standards. During the following year only 4 new buses made their debut, these being Leyland PD2/12s, 2 of which had Roe 'Beverley Bar' highbridge bodies, the other 2 being fitted with lowbridge bodywork by this same coachbuilder.

The main event of 1955 was the purchase of Wilson & Hughes business at Bridlington which further consolidated the company's position in that seaside town.

The origins of Wilson & Hughes dated back to 1920 when Jack Wilson, a scrap metal merchant, formed a partnership with Billy Hughes, a professional boxer, and purchased a Lancia charabanc. This was initially used on private hire work but after three months, they decided to operate a town service in Bridlington and for this purchased a Ford model T. Expansion in 1922 with the acquisition of another Lancia and a Chevrolet led them to seek premises in which to keep and maintain their vehicles and later in that same year a base was opened in Kirkgate, Bridlington for this purpose. By now, the fleet name 'White Bus Company' had been adopted and, as was the vogue at that time, each charabanc was given a name (Leading Lady; Better Times; Happy Hours etc.). In April 1926 a route was opened from Princes Street, Bridlington to Flamborouigh in competition with Archer Robinson and Blue Bus Services and by 1929 a second garage had been acquired, this being in Moorfield Road. When Blue Bus Services sold out to Scarborough & District in January 1930, Wilson & Hughes took over their office in Queen Street and altered their Flamborough service to start from this point.

By 1939, Bedfords, Commers, Gilfords, an Albion and a Dodge had joined the fleet (all of which were acquired secondhand) and during the war numerous contracts were undertaken for the transportation of personnel to airfields at Catfoss, Carnaby and Lisset and for a period, 4 buses were also loaned to Wallace Arnold Tours. When Bridlington Corporation opened Bessingby Hall at Sewerby to the public soon after the war, White Bus Co. found its popularity such that larger capacity vehicles were needed to serve this park which was coincidentally on their Flamborough route. To this end, 2 Leyland TD2s with Roe centre-entrance highbridge bodywork were purchased in June 1947 from Enterprise & Silver Dawn of Scunthorpe, although only one of these was placed in service. A third double decker arrived in November, this also being a Leyland TD2 with Roe highbridge bodywork - but this time with conventional rear platform - purchased

from G.Ennifer of Doncaster. The TD2s were to enjoy only a short life with their new owner however and in July 1950 a Park Royal highbridge-bodied AEC Regent was bought from Halifax Corporation, being joined during the following year by a further two Regents from this same source, albeit on this occasion with Roe bodywork. Finally, the need for additional double deckers produced a trio of ex.London Transport Daimler CWA6s in July 1953, one of which was immediately painted into its new owner's white livery with red relief and placed in service, one being stored until July 1955 before making its debut and the other never entering service with White Bus Co. By this time, a garage was also maintained in Stepney Grove, Bridlington.

East Yorkshire, who paid £14,500 for White Bus Co., took over their licences, buses and depots on 11 November 1955, and although 10 vehicles were included in the deal (2 Leyland Cubs; 2 Bedford OWBs; 1 AEC Regal; 2 AEC Regents and 3 Daimler CWA6s), only the 3 Daimlers were taken into East Yorkshire stock, the remaining 7 being sold in March 1956. None of the three depots at Bridlington or the dormy shed at Flamborough were used by East Yorkshire and one of the acquired Daimlers reclined in store until its eventual sale in November 1956.

Negotiations for the purchase of some houses at the rear of Bridlington bus station were successfully completed in February 1956 and two months later, a further plot of land adjacent to Westwood bus station at Scarborough was leased from the BTC to enable the company to extend their vehicle parking area. Still on the subject of property, the new depot at Railway Street, Pocklington was opened on 1 May whilst the rebuilding of Elloughton garage was also completed.

All the new buses delivered to East Yorkshire in 1956 were AEC Regent Vs with exposed radiators and Willowbrook

New in 1946 to London Transport, Duple-bodied Daimler CWA6 HGC279 was one of three such buses acquired with the business of Wilson & Hughes (White Bus Service), Bridlington in 1955. Seen here in Bridlington bus station in 1956, 665 had by that time been given full East Yorkshire livery.

Above : One of a pair of lowbridge Roe-bodied Leyland PD2/12s purchased in 1955, 632 is seen here leaving Bridlington bus station on a journey to Hornsea via Beeford in 1962.

'Beverley Bar' highbridge bodies and on this occasion, rear platform doors were incorporated into their design. Totalling 15, all entered service in November. Two conversions were also undertaken towards the end of the year, both involving ex.Everingham vehicles. One of these, a 1947 AEC Regal, was made into a breakdown wagon whilst the other, a Barnaby-rebodied Daimler CWG5 was transformed into a left luggage office for seasonal use at Westwood bus station, Scarborough.

1957 saw the arrival of the last 'traditional' Beverley Bar-roofed double deckers, these being a pair of AEC Regent Vs with concealed radiators and Roe bodywork fitted with rear platform doors. Joining these were two exposed radiator AEC Regent Vs with Willowbrook lowbridge bodywork (for use in the Goole area); 5 Harrington-bodied Leyland PSUC1/2 coaches and 4 Park Royal-bodied front entrance 39-seat Leyland PSUC1/1 buses. The latter were equipped for one-person-operation and were the first buses in the fleet thus fitted. Following East Yorkshire's tradition, the new coaches were all given names - Humber Star; Dales Star; Wold Star; Buckrose Star and Hunsley Star.

Like many other bus operators at that time, East Yorkshire found themselves suffering from rising costs and falling receipts and as a result began to seek various ways of making economies. This led to reducing the frequencies on a number of routes which according to projections would save around £11,000 per annum and in June 1958, after finding

Below : The last conventional lowbridge double deckers to join the East Yorkshire fleet were a pair of Willowbrook-bodied AEC Regent Vs which made their debut in January 1957. 650 is seen here on a Hull local service in 1965.

the former Everingham's route from Pocklington to York via Stamford Bridge being extremely unprofitable, they agreed to sell this to Baileys of Fangfoss for £100 subject to safeguards being given to East Yorkshire over certain parts of the route. Baileys took over this operation in July. A few weeks later, on 16 August, the new Driffield depot was opened to replace the old premises in the town and incorporated into this was a new enquiry/booking office.

The year did however see one notable event - the 25th. anniversary of the Hull Co-ordination Agreement. This was celebrated at a function when the East Yorkshire Board presented to the City Council a model bus, made of silver and accurately representing a Leyland Tiger Cub with Weymann bodywork. The design was however unique - the

Standing in Westwood bus station Scarborough at the start of its long journey to Hull is 646, a Willowbrook-bodied AEC Regent V of 1956 vintage which in addition to sporting a traditional AEC exposed radiator was given the added luxury of rear platform doors.

*Previous page.*

*Top to bottom, left column :*

*1949 Roe-bodied Leyland PD1A 491 (JAT459) arrives at Westwood bus station, Scarborough on a journey from Bridlington in 1963 and despite its age, still looks immaculate in its dark blue & primrose livery. (T.Godfrey)*

*Still sporting its cream & black livery, Cherry of Beverley's former Strathclyde PTE Alexander-bodied Leyland Atlantean KSU856P rests at Morton Lane, Beverley after working a schools contract. (J.Whiteing)*

*Pictured operating a Scarborough town service is Scarborough & District ECW-bodied Bristol RESL6G 158 (JHN558K), a single decker inherited from United with the company's Scarborough operations in 1986. (P.J.S.Shipp)*

*Resting at Beverley still wearing the NBC green livery in which it was received from Devon General in 1986 is 922 (LOD722P), an ECW-bodied Bristol VRT. (EYMS)*

*Top to bottom, right column :*

*Beverley Bar roofed 8ft wide Roe-bodied Leyland PD2/3 548 stands alongside Park Royal-bodied AEC Bridgemaster 699 at Ferensway bus park, Hull in 1965. (T.Godfrey)*

*Freshly repainted in NBC poppy red livery with a single white relief band, Park Royal-bodied Daimler Fleetline 868 collects its Hull-bound passengers at Beverley bus station on 3 September 1982. (J.Whiteing)*

*Sporting an interim style of Scarborough & District fleet name and logo is 793 (SGR793V), an ECW-bodied Bristol VRT inherited from United with the Scarborough operations in 1986. Still wearing NBC poppy red livery, it is seen working a Scarborough town service in July 1988 (S.A.Jenkinson)*

*Amongst the buses taken over with the business of Phillips, Shiptonthorpe was this former Tyne & Wear PTE/Burnley & Pendle MCCW-bodied Bristol RELL6G JBR102F. (P.J.S.Shipp)*

*Acquired with the business of Everingham Bros. in 1953, Barnaby-bodied AEC Regal EWF54 was converted into a breakdown wagon for East Yorkshire in 1956. It served for a further twelve years in its new role before being scrapped in March 1968.*

mouldings on one side representing the East Yorkshire livery and fleet name while those on the other depicted the Hull City Transport style with its well-known 'side flash'. This item is still on display in Hull's Guildhall alongside other gifts to the city.

Only three new buses were placed in service in 1958, one of which was a Park Royal-bodied Albion Aberdonian 39-seater of 7ft.6in. width which had been purchased for use on the narrow roads around Pocklington. The other 2 were Leyland PSUC1/1s with Park Royal 39-seat front entrance bodies which had in fact been delivered in September/October of the previous year but had remained in store prior to making their debut in the spring of 1958. During June, one

of the 1948 Leyland PS1 saloons was converted into a stores lorry and was also equipped for tree lopping for use when such duties were necessary.

1959 proved to be a barren year as far as the fleet was concerned, with no new vehicles being placed in service. The only change of note was the conversion of 590-605, the 1952 Weymann-bodied Leyland PSU1/13s, from rear to front entrance to make them suitable for one-person-operation. Remaining as 42-seaters, the conversions were carried out by Chas.H.Roe between July 1959 and May 1962 at a cost of £3,850.

As if making up for the lack of new vehicles in 1959, no fewer than 20 were placed in service during the following year. These comprised 4 AEC Bridgemasters with Park Royal rear entrance bodywork incorporating platform doors and 16 Leyland Tiger Cubs of which 8 had MCCW 41-seat dual purpose bodywork, 4 had MCCW 41-seat bus bodies and 4 had Harrington 35-seat coach bodies. The latter were given the names 'Pocklington Star; Holderness Star; Driffield Star and Middleton Star' whilst the Bridgemasters which did not have any modification to their roofs were as a result unable to pass under Beverley Bar.

1960 also saw the Fawdon Omnibus Co.Ltd. going into voluntary liquidation, and as a consequence of this, East

*In 1958 East Yorkshire bought a solitary Albion Aberdonian with 7ft.6in. wide Park Royal body for use on its rural services which negotiated narrow roads. On this occasion however, it is seen at Westwood bus station, Scarborough operating the Hunmanby service.*

*Next page*

*Top to bottom, left column :*

*Seen on a journey to Malton while wearing its experimental livery which incorporated a cream roof is ECW-bodied Bristol VRT 974 (UKH974R).    (EYMS)*

*Painted in Scarborough & District's Yorkshire Coastliner livery, Willowbrook-bodied Leyland Leopard 207 stands in Valley Bridge bus station, Scarborough on 6 July 1988. (K.A.Jenkinson)*

*Repainted for a short time into Wallace Arnold colours but omitting that operator's 'WA' logo was East Yorkshire's Leyland Royal Tiger Doyen 7 (3277KH, originally A107OKH).   (EYMS)*

*191 (1918KH), a Plaxton-bodied Leyland Leopard still wears its East Yorkshire white & two tone blue livery - albeit with Cherry's fleet names - soon after its transfer to the Cherry fleet.    (P.J.S.Shipp)*

*Top to bottom, right column :*

*Scarborough & District Plaxton Paramount-bodied Volvo B10M 48 (B930MLN) was one of a trio purchased secondhand from Capital Coaches, West Drayton in 1988. Named 'Wold Star', it is seen here in Bradford on a private hire duty in August 1990.   (K.A.Jenkinson)*

*Painted in an all-over advertising livery, Scarborough & District's ex.Northern General dual door ECW-bodied Leyland Atlantean 610 (NCN110L) is seen here at Corner Cafe, Scarborough while working the sea-front service. As can be seen, although it retains its front and rear roof domes, it has been converted to open-top configuration by the removal of the centre section of its roof.   (B.Newsome)*

*KHH573W, a Reeve Burgess 12-seat Mercedes L307D was acquired with the business of Phoenix Taxis in 1987 and then placed in the Cherry's fleet. It is seen here still wearing Phoenix livery.   (EYMS)*

*Hired from Lincolnshire Road Car Co. to alleviate a vehicle shortage, Plaxton-bodied Briatol RELH6L 1437 (URC960M) is pictured here while operating in the Cherry's fleet, the name of which is carried in its windscreens.   (P.J.S.Shipp)*

*Park Royal-bodied AEC Bridgemaster demonstrator 9JML was evaluated by East Yorkshire in the spring of 1957. It is seen here in Cottingham Road whilst operating the Hull - Cottingham service in April of that year.*

Street, Pocklington, which had been sold some years earlier and then leased back to the company, was modernised during 1963 as was Bridlington bus station following the completion of its extension to give the company the extra space they needed in this seaside resort. In February talks opened with United Automobile Services regarding the company's joint use of United's bus station at Valley Bridge, Scarborough as an eventual replacement for their Westwood site, but these proved inconclusive and East Yorkshire had to continue to use their own bus station for several more years. The land in Collier Street, Hull which had been purchased from the railways on 1 January 1963 was sold a year later to Hull Corporation after agreement had been reached regarding its future development.

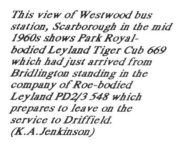

*This view of Westwood bus station, Scarborough in the mid 1960s shows Park Royal-bodied Leyland Tiger Cub 669 which had just arrived from Bridlington standing in the company of Roe-bodied Leyland PD2/3 548 which prepares to leave on the service to Driffield. (K.A.Jenkinson)*

Yorkshire received payment for the 505 shares it held in this company.

A total of 16 more Park Royal-bodied AEC Bridgemasters arrived in 1961 and in addition to being fitted with rear platform doors, these also had the upper deck above the base rail of their windows tapered inwards to allow them to successfully pass through the Gothic arch of Beverley Bar. These were followed in 1962 by a further 15 Bridgemasters with tapered top decks, although these differed from their predecessors by having their entrance at the front instead of at the rear. Joining these in 1962 were 7 Willowbrook-bodied 47-seat dual purpose Leyland Leopard PSU3/3Rs which sported an attractive light-blue livery with primrose relief.

On 1 January 1963, the railway interest in East Yorkshire passed from the British Transport Commission to the newly-formed Transport Holding Company, although there was no noticable effect of this in the running of the company. The former Everingham Bros. booking office at 12 Railway

Hull city centre which had for many years been an area of growing traffic congestion had been under the planner's gaze for some considerable time and after much discussion with all the parties concerned, it was decided to introduce a massive one-way traffic system during 1964. This came into effect on 26 June and as a result, many of the company's services had to be re-routed to make their way to and from Ferensway Coach Station. Although initially this caused the traffic office a great deal of extra work, the result of the new one-way system proved beneficial to East Yorkshire as it assisted schedules to be maintained, especially during peak hours.

In 1964, 10 more front entrance Park Royal-bodied AEC double deckers with specially tapered bodywork made their debut, although these were based on the new low-height Renown chassis which had been introduced as a replacement for the Bridgemaster. Also arriving were another 7 dual purpose Willowbrook-bodied 47-seat Leyland

After giving East Yorkshire ten years service as a single deck bus, Brush-bodied Leyland PS1 467 was rebuilt by the company as a stores/towing lorry in 1958, a role it continued to perform until it was sold for preservation in 1973.

Leopards. The following year produced a further 14 AEC Renowns identical to those delivered in 1964 and 10 Weymann-bodied 49-seat Leyland Leopard buses, the bodies of which were built to B.E.T. standard specification.

Following the announcement towards the end of 1964 by British Railways of their proposed closure of their Hull - Hornsea and Hull - Withernsea services, East Yorkshire applied for a licence to operate new road services between these points. Despite objections being lodged by Hornsea UDC in respect of the first mentioned service and Connor & Graham of Easington in respect of the latter, the company was granted licences for both routes on a one-year trial basis. Before operations began, East Yorkshire applied in the spring of 1965 for a licence for a new circular service to operate in both directions from Ferensway Coach Station, Hull to Hessle Square, Anlaby, Willerby and Cottingham.

Of the twelve MCCW-bodied Leyland Tiger Cubs joining the fleet in 1960, eight - including 686 - were fitted with coach-type seats and painted in a primrose livery with riviera blue window surrounds for use on long distance services.

Above : The remaining four of the 1960 MCCW-bodied Leyland Tiger Cubs were fitted with bus seats and were painted in the company's smart indigo blue & primrose livery as illustrated by 691 when only a few months old.

One of three Harrington bodied Leyland Tiger Cub coaches purchased in 1957, 677 was named 'Wold Star' and is seen here in its attractive primrose & riviera blue livery whilst employed on touring duties in 1965.

*The last Harrington-bodied coaches to be purchased by East Yorkshire were four Leyland Tiger Cubs which made their debut in 1960. One of these, 693 was named 'Holderness Star' and is seen here while operating an extended tour.*

*The first AEC Bridgemasters to be purchased by East Yorkshire were four Park Royal-bodied examples which made their debut in 1960 and were the only buses of this type added to the fleet which did not have their upper decks tapered inward to allow easy passage beneath Beverley Bar. As can be seen by the photograph of 699 (above right), they were still able to negotiate the 'Bar' with care. On the right, 697 is pictured passing through Hull in the indigo blue & primrose livery in which it was delivered.*

Upon the granting of this, services 8 (Hull - Hessle Square) and 60 (Hull - Setting Dyke Estate), which were covered by the new circular operation, were withdrawn. At this same time an application was also made for a service to operate jointly with Hull City Transport from Ferensway to Mizzen Road via Beverley Road, and later in the year another route jointly operated with Hull City Transport was started from Ferensway to Pickering Road/Hessle Road. Before the year ended, consequent upon the withdrawal of the rail passenger services between Beverley and York, East Yorkshire on 30 November began operation of a new thrice-daily service between Ferenaway Coach Station, Hull and Rougier Street York. Numbered 46X it ran on a limited stop basis calling only at Cottingham, Beverley, Market Weighton, Shiptonthorpe and Pocklington.

*Willowbrook dual purpose-bodied Leyland Leopard 733 pictured here in its original Riviera blue & primrose livery leaves Rougier Street, York on its way to Bridlington in 1964.*

*Park Royal-bodied AEC Bridgemaster 711 had its upper deck windows tapered inward to allow it passage beneath Beverley Bar. Seen at Hull in 1973, a year before its withdrawal from service, it sports NBC logos and corporate-style fleet name.*

The last of the AEC Renowns to be purchased arrived in 1966, all 10 having Park Royal front entrance bodywork with tapered top decks. Also making their debut were 15 rear-engined Leyland Panther single deckers with Marshall 49-seat BET-style bodies, and although these proved somewhat troublesome throughout their lives some gave 14-years service before being finally withdrawn. At the start of the year, one of the 1950 Roe-bodied Leyland PD2/3

*The last Park Royal-bodied AEC Bridgemasters to join the fleet did so in 1963 and were of front entrance layout with specially tapered top deck windows. Seen when comparatively new, 755 leaves Hull city centre on a journey to Hessle Square.*

*Making its debut in 1964, Willowbrook-bodied dual-purpose Leyland Leopard 773 differed from the 1962 vehicles of this combination by having double curvature windscreens. Painted in riviera blue & primrose livery it is seen here before working a journey from Birmingham to Hull.*

double deckers - 541 - was converted into a left luggage office for use at Scarborough's Westwood bus station where it replaced the former Everingham Bros. Daimler which had served in this capacity since 1957.

Although a new route, jointly operated with Hull City Transport, from Hull to Willerby via Kirkella had been planned to start on 17 January 1966, its commencement had to be delayed due to the Traffic Commissioner deferring his decision in respect of City Transport's involvement, despite

*Amongst the last AEC Renowns to remain in service was Park Royal forward-entrance bodied 787 of 1966 vintage. It is seen here in NBC poppy red & white livery operating a Hull local route during 1979, its final year in service. (J.Fozard)*

East Yorkshire's application having already been granted. Before this saga had been resolved, the company was allowed a short-term licence for a new express service from Ferensway Coach Station to Brough Airfield to connect with an air service by Autair International Airways to Luton. This was a somewhat unusual operation as a condition of the licence allowed the service to be diverted to Leconfield or Holme on Spalding Moor airfields on occasions when the weather rendered Brough unfit for the air service. Soon after this new service began, East Yorkshire extended their 46X Hull - York express service from its former terminus at Rougier Street to York railway station.

In an attempt to counter continually rising costs and falling receipts, further operating economies were being actively sought by the company and in February 1967 a scheme was drawn up and submitted to the Traffic Commissioners for approval. Unfortunately, the plans in question were not accepted and thus when service cuts were implemented on 16 April 1967 they were less severe than had been originally intended. Nevertheless, these service reductions resulted in a saving of some 358,000 operational miles and £29,000 per annum.

After suffering severe fire damage at Market Weighton in June 1967, Windover-bodied Leyland Royal Tiger coach 614 was prematurely withdrawn and two months later, its blackened remains were dismantled at the company's Anlaby Common workshops.

The first rear-engined double deckers to be purchased by the company took up their duties on 1 December 1967. These were 4 Daimler Fleetlines with Gardner 6LX engines and Park Royal 68-seat bodies, the upper portion of which was suitably inward-tapered to allow passage beneath Beverley Bar. Joining these were a pair of Leyland Panthers which were fitted with 44-seat coach bodies by MCCW.

1968 witnessed the arrival of a further 14 Park Royal-bodied Daimler Fleetlines identical to those making their debut in the final month of the previous year, and 23 single deckers of which 4 were Leyland Panthers with Marshall dual purpose bodies, 3 were Panthers with 44-seat Plaxton coach bodies and 16 were Panther Cubs with Marshall 45-seat bus bodywork. Although these allowed the withdrawal of a number of older vehicles, 5 of the 1957/8 Park Royal-bodied Leyland Tiger Cubs were overhauled, repainted and recertified and then immediately placed in store where they remained until September 1971 when all were sold without having re-entered service.

During the early part of 1968 East Yorkshire purchased the licence for a service between Melbourne and Selby from W.Gorwood of East Cottingwith. W.Gorwood had started in business in the early 1900s as a horse-bus operator with a service from East Cottingwith to York, eventually converting this to motor bus operation and adding various other services to York and Selby. Despite selling his Selby licence to East Yorkshire as stated above, Gorwood continued to operate his two other services and still remains in business today. No vehicles passed to East Yorkshire on this occasion.

Following the completion of negotiations for British Electric Traction to sell their United Kingdom passenger transport interests to the State in 1968, its shareholdings in its subsidiaries were taken over by the Transport Holding Company as from 1 March 1968 and this brought East Yorkshire into single ownership for the first time in its history. Its new masters changed yet again (if only in title) on 1 January 1969 when the National Bus Company took over the interests of the THC.

Although the company had rented a garage at Beverley from the various railway authorities since 1932, the option to purchase was not taken up until 1 September 1966, this leading to the garage and land freehold being conveyanced to East Yorkshire on 9 December 1968.

Returning to the fleet, during the summer of 1968 one of the full-fronted Leyland PD2/12 double deck coaches which had latterly been downgraded for bus duties entered Anlaby Common workshops for conversion into a new breakdown wagon, and when completed in September it replaced the ex.Everingham Bros, AEC Regal which had previously served in this capacity.

7 more Park Royal-bodied 'tapered top' Fleetline double deckers entered service in May 1969 as did 2 36-seat Plaxton coach-bodied Leyland Leopards and 7 Marshall dual purpose-bodied Leopards. The solitary Albion Aberdonian which, since its arrival in January 1958 had proved troublesome and unpopular with staff, was converted into a luggage office for use at Scarborough's Westwood bus station, taking up its new duties in July 1969.

As a consequence of the reduction in population of Hull's central area and the increase on the newer housing estates affecting the 'B' area revenue, the co-ordination agreement between the company and Hull City Council was revised on 28 December 1969, this resulting in the company having to

contribute the 'B' portion of their country routes to the 'pool'. During the following year, agreement was reached with the Corporation for East Yorkshire staff to use the latter's canteen facilities at Lombard Street, thus allowing the closure of the company's old canteen at Ferensway Coach Station, Hull.

The vexed question of the future of Westwood bus station at Scarborough was finally resolved in 1970 when, after further discussions with United Automobile Services (who were now also under National Bus Company control), agreement was reached for East Yorkshire to terminate their Scarborough services at United's Valley Bridge bus station, commencing in May. Thereafter, Westwood was retained as a bus park and for certain express services, the only stage carriage operations still terminating there being those operated by Hardwicks Services who although not known at that time were to join the East Yorkshire fold some seventeen years later. Undoubtedly the most important aspect of 1970 as far as East Yorkshire was concerned was the opening of a new road in Beverley which circumnavigated the famous Gothic arch. As mentioned several times earlier, this arch had caused the company to purchase double deckers with specially-shaped roofs since 1934, and the opening of this new road must have caused East Yorkshire much rejoicing as well as a great deal of relief.

In preparation for Britain's conversion to decimal currency on 15 February 1971, the company purchased 260 Mk.II Setright single area decimal ticket machines for delivery that

*The only new coach to join the fleet in 1971 was 894, a 40-seat Plaxton-bodied Leyland Leopard which was to be used on the company's extended tours. Wearing its attractive riviera blue & primrose livery, it is seen here on one such duty in Eire during the summer of 1971. (EYMS)*

*884, a full-height Alexander-bodied Daimler Fleetline was one of ten placed in service in 1971 and is seen here during the following year after being repainted into the short-lived NBC-style indigo blue & white livery to which corporate-style fleet names were added.*

*One of five low-height Alexander-bodied Leyland Atlanteans diverted to East Yorkshire from Western Welsh in 1971, 898 was one of the last new buses to enter service in the original indigo blue & primrose livery. Unusually, these five buses did not carry a white band on their roofs like all the company's other double deckers.*

month, the cost of these being a staggering £22,500. These were used to replace the old Willebrew ticketing system which was thought by the company to be unsuitable for future use.

At a board meeting early in the year it was agreed to offer for sale some land owned by the company at Cottingham but to retain that, together with buildings, at Memorial Avenue, Withernsea. Arrangements were also made to obtain 5 Leyland PDR1/3 Atlantean double deckers from Western Welsh for £45,000, and in September the directors agreed that 10 additional double deckers suitable for one person operation should be obtained as soon as available from other NBC subsidiaries. This order was however cancelled in November in favour of 10 AEC Renowns being exchanged for Daimler Fleetlines from Northern General Transport Co. Ltd.

No new vehicles had joined the fleet during 1970, but during the following year 2 49-seat Willowbrook dual purpose-bodied Leopards, 1 Plaxton 40-seat coach-bodied Leopard, 10 Alexander-bodied Daimler Fleetlines and 5 Alexander-bodied Leyland Atlanteans were received. The Fleetlines had conventionally-shaped roofs as a result of them no longer having a need to pass through Beverley Bar whilst the Atlanteans were diverted from Western Welsh to whom 4 had been delivered and registered VUH 382-5J but had not been used, the fifth coming direct to East Yorkshire. Before being placed in service by their new owner, VUH382-5J were re-registered AAT395/7-9K. In December, Roe lowbridge-bodied Leyland PD2/12 633 was converted into a permanent driver training vehicle.

*Weymann-bodied 919 was one of twenty Daimler Fleetlines acquired from Tynemouth & District in 1972 in exchange for AEC Renowns. Painted in East Yorkshire's indigo blue & primrose livery with a white roof, it is seen here working a Hull local service in 1973.*

During 1972, although a total of 25 vehicles was taken into stock, only 5 of these (Plaxton-bodied Leopard coaches) were new, the remaining 20 being Daimler Fleetline double deckers obtained from Northern General. Of these, 10 dated from 1963 and had Weymann bodywork, 7 were new in 1965 and had Alexander bodies and 3 were of 1967 vintage and also carried bodywork by Alexander. All 20 had previously been operated in Northern's Tynemouth & District fleet and all except one entered service with their new owner in East Yorkshire's attractive indigo blue & primrose colours, being the last vehicles so to do. The remaining one was painted in the new NBC-style blue & white colour scheme which was not nearly so attractive. In exchange, East Yorkshire despatched 6 of their AEC Renowns to Northern General in January for use in their Tynemouth fleet. Further departures included 5 of the 1960 MCCW-bodied Tiger Cubs which were sold to United Counties Omnibus Co.Ltd. for further use. Other withdrawals saw the demise of the last of the double deckers with traditional 'Beverley Bar' roofs, although the 'tapered top' Bridgemasters, Renowns and Fleetlines continued to be active in the fleet. Indeed, one example still remained in service in 1991.

Following an edict by the National Bus Company that their subsidiaries' individual liveries all had to be abandoned in favour of a new corporate colour scheme, East Yorkshire painted their first vehicle - 798, a Marshall-bodied Panther - in the new NBC blue & white hue in September 1972 and for a few months, all subsequent repaints were out-shopped in this manner. In March, the compant transferred its 4,000 shares in London Coastal Coaches to other NBC interests and at the same time passed their 3,200 shares in Blackpool Omnibus Stations Ltd. to Ribble Motor Services at Preston.

The revised co-ordination scheme in Hull which had come into effect on 29 December 1969 giving East Yorkshire 30% of the joint revenue was further modified on 1 April 1973 to reflect more accurately the mileage worked by each of the two partners, thus ensuring the continuation of this long-lasting scheme. Prior to this, a surprise move early in the year saw the acquisition on 25 January of a stage carriage licence for a service from Driffield to Scarborough via West Lutton. Taken over from Downes of Weaverthorpe, this service operated only on Thursday of each week and no vehicles were involved in the deal. A.Downes had set up in business in May 1930 and it was not until June 1945 his business grew beyond one vehicle. The business was later re-formed by Miriam Hannah, Joseph Arthur, Leslie and Thomas Henry Downes trading as M.H.Downes & Sons and the service passing to East Yorkshire (numbered 35 by its new operator) was eventually discontinued in May 1977.

1973 saw the introduction to the fleet of the first Bristols to be operated by East Yorkshire when between January and July 8 ECW-bodied VRT double deckers were received. All sported the new NBC corporate blue & white livery - surprisingly with the addition of East Yorkshire's unique

*Leaving Anne Street, Hull on its way to Elloughton is one of East Yorkshire's 1974 ECW Bristol VRTs, 935, which was one of the first to be delivered new in NBC poppy red & white livery.*

*Approaching the coach interchange at Charlotte Road, Sheffield enroute to London on 2 October 1980 is 164, a five-year old Plaxton-bodied Leyland Leopard painted in NBC's corporate white coach livery. (K.A.Jenkinson)*

*One of five Duple Dominant bus-bodied Ford R1014s purchased new in 1976 for use on the company's rural services, 170 which was numerically the first is seen here operating the 33A service to Driffield in 1978.*

white roof band - and one, 932, was fitted with a prototype two-height entrance platform which it retained until August 1980 when a more conventional platform was fitted. A further 10 Bristol VRTs were purchased in 1974 together with 15 Park Royal-bodied Leyland AN68/1R Atlanteans which were of 14ft.6in height (the VRTs being 13ft.8in.high). Following a directive received from NBC's London headquarters informing operators that the corporate blue livery had now been withdrawn from the options, and that only the choice of poppy red & white or leaf green & white remained, East Yorkshire reluctantly decided upon the former as its new 'enforced' livery and as a result started to repaint their fleet into their new colour in January 1974. All the new Bristol VRTs and Atlanteans joining the fleet in his year were received in poppy red, although after only five months in service, new Atlantean 948 was repainted into an all-over advertising scheme for Andymans D.I.Y. Superstore to become the first bus in the fleet to be adorned in this manner.

A significant event in August 1974 was the resignation from the Board, on his retirement, of C.R.H.Wreathall, whose father had been one of the first directors in 1926 and who had been known throughout the bus industry because of his unique style and his association with East Yorkshire for very many years.

1975 brought more secondhand vehicles into the fleet in the form of 7 Leyland Leopard coaches, 5 of which were Alexander-bodied and came from National Travel North West having been new to North Western Road Car Co., the other two being Plaxton-bodied examples from United, one having been new to Shaw Bros. of Byers Green, the other ordered

by Wilkinsons of Sedgefield before their acquisition by United. The only new vehicles to join the fleet were 4 Plaxton-bodied Leopard coaches, two entering service in december, the remaining pair not making their debut until February 1976.

Finding themselves with a small surplus of dual purpose single deckers, East Yorkshire were able to loan a number of these to other NBC operators towards the end of the year to help them to overcome vehicle shortages. The first of these

*Acquired from United Automobile Services in 1975, Plaxton-bodied Leyland Leopard 160 (NHN415E) which had been ordered by Wilkinsons of Sedgefield before their take-over by United sadly ended its days in August 1979 when it was destroyed by fire.*

*Amongst the first Leyland Nationals to be purchased by East Yorkshire was 169 which entered service in September 1976. Seen here in its original NBC poppy red & white livery, it was on its way to Hull's Fleet Estate on the 56A service which in more recent times has been operated by Routemasters.   (I.C.Gibbs)*

*One of five Alexander-bodied Leyland Leopard coaches acquired from National Travel (West) in 1977, National white-liveried 37 (JDB237E) is seen here soon after joining the East Yorkshire fleet.   (J.Whiteing)*

*One of five Alexander-bodied Leyland Leopards acquired from National Travel (West) in 1977, 41 (JDB241E) was repainted into NBC 'local coach' poppy red & white livery in April 1979 and is seen later that year on a stage carriage duty from Hull to Little Weighton.*

were a pair of Willowbrook-bodied Leopards of 1962 vintage which were loaned to Yorkshire Woollen District Transport in September. One of these returned home in November whilst

the other was subsequently sold to Yorkshire W.D. in December. Following on the heels of these were 6 similar vehicles which in October were loaned to Northern General Transport Co. Ltd. All but one of these were purchased by Northern before the end of the year, the odd one out returning to East Yorkshire in May 1976 only to be sold to Northern two months later. Earlier in the year a Willowbrook dual purpose bodied Leopard and a Willowbrook bus-bodied Leopard had been sold to United in exchange for the two Leopard coaches mentioned earlier.

In Beverley, a new bus station was opened at Sow Hill where East Yorkshire erected an information office, this relieving the town's Market Place of its growing congestion and providing passengers with much-needed better facilities.

A total of 21 new vehicles were taken into stock in 1976 and amongst these were the first Fords in the post-war fleet. These comprised 5 Duple Dominant bus-bodied 43-seat R1014s which were used almost exclusively by Driffield and Pocklington depots. The other new vehicles were 3 Plaxton-bodied Leyland Leopard coaches, 8 ECW-bodied Bristol VRTs with Leyland 501 engines and the first Leyland Nationals to join the fleet - 5 11.3m examples with single door 49-seat bodywork. Prior to the arrival of the latter, a Leyland National was received on loan from West Yorkshire Road Car Co. Ltd. in order to familiarise drivers with this new type of bus. In exchange for this, East Yorkshire sent one of its 1969 Marshall-bodied Leopards to West Yorkshire from May until July. Amongst the vehicles leaving the fleet were 3 of the Harrington-bodied Leopard coaches which were despatched to the new NBC disposal pool at Bracebridge Heath, Lincoln in March where they were joined later in the year by the two 1967 MCCW-bodied Leyland PSUR1/2R coaches and one of the ex.Northern general Fleetlines. In addition, during July 5 Willowbrook dual purpose-bodied Leopards were sold to Northern General and 5 AEC Bridgemasters to United. Only one of the latter was placed in service in its new home however - and then only for a solitary day - and following the cancellation of this sale, the 5 buses concerned were all placed in store by United who later in the year sold them on East Yorkshire's behalf. Finally, during 1976, the blue livery finally faded into extinction when, in February, Park Royal-bodied Fleetline 870 succumbed to the new poppy red & white corporate NBC colour scheme.

Another 15 ECW-bodied Bristol VRTs were delivered to the company during 1977, one of which was despatched direct from Lowestoft to United Automobile Services in March, operating for that company until May when it was eventually sent to join its sisters at Hull. A further 5 Alexander-bodied Leopard coaches, new to North Western Road Car Co. in 1967/8 were acquired from National Travel West in December, although these, painted in NBC's corporate white coach livery, did not enter service with their new owner until March of the following year. More bus-bodied Leopards and ex.Northern General Fleetlines were despatched to the NBC disposal pool at Lincoln during the year for cannibalisation whilst a pair of Weymann B49F-bodied Leopards were sold to United in May. One of the rear entrance AEC Bridgemasters of 1961 vintage was converted into a tree lopper in the company's Anlaby Common workshops during July while in September, a two-year old Leopard coach was so badly damaged in an accident on its way to Scotland that its body had to be scrapped and its chassis despatched to Plaxtons for fitting with a new 47-seat body. It eventually returned to service in May 1978.

East Yorkshire did not receive any further new vehicles until September 1978 when 4 B-series 'short' 41-seat Leyland Nationals made their debut together with a Plaxton coach-bodied Leopard of which type 2 more followed in November/December. The final month of the year witnessed the arrival of another 4 Leyland-engined Bristol VRT, although unlike the previous deliveries, these were fitted with ECW bodywork of 14ft. 6in. height. Only one secondhand vehicle was purchased during the year, this being a Willowbrook dual purpose-bodied Leopard coach which had been sold by the company to United in February 1975. Following its re-purchase in March 1978, it was stored for

*Park Royal-bodied AEC Bridgemaster 710, its passenger-carrying days having ended, was converted to a tree-lopper in 1977 and painted into NBC-style poppy red livery. (EYMS)*

*Full-height ECW-bodied, Leyland-engined Bristol VRT 987 is seen here wearing an experimental livery of poppy red with white lower deck window frames during the mid 'eighties. (EYMS)*

two months before re-entering service with its original fleet number (882).

Despite Bridlington having a sea-front which was ideally suited for open-top double deck operation, no such vehicles had existed in the fleet since the start of World War II when the three open-top Leyland TD1s had been withdrawn from service. It was thus surprising when, in July 1978, the company decided to re-introduce open-top operations to this seaside resort. Having no vehicles of this type themselves, and being unsure of the success of such a service, East Yorkshire decided to test the water by hiring a pair of open top double deckers with which to conduct this experiment. One of the buses received on loan was a Bristol LD6G Lodekka from Southern Vectis which retained its owner's green & white livery but was given East Yorkshire fleet number 101. The other was a 30ft. long LDL6G Lodekka hired from Western National which sported a red & white colour scheme and carried the name 'Admiral Boscawen' and was given fleet number 102 by its new temporary operator. Both were employed in Bridlington from July until the end of the summer season in September, after which time they were returned to their rightful owners. So successful was this operation, that East Yorkshire decided to convert two of their own vehicles to open-top configuration for use during 1979 and for this purpose selected a pair of the ex. Tynemouth Alexander-bodied Fleetlines, the first of which entered

*Named 'Sewerby Star' and adorned with east Yorkshire Coaster fleet names, Alexander-bodied Daimler Fleetline 901 (AFT784C) was acquired from Tynemouth & District in 1972 in conventional closed-top form and was converted to open-top configuration in 1979. It is seen here in Bridlington in 1980 wearing a colourful orange & blue livery.*

*Full-height Leyland-engined ECW-bodied Bristol VRT 988 in NBC poppy red & white livery had 'Breakaway Express' vinyls applied below its destnation screen and in front of its fleet names for use on the 801 coastal service in the early 'eighties. (EYMS)*

*Plaxton-bodied Leyland Leopard 197 (KGK477K) was new to Samuelson's New Transport Co., London in 1971 and later passed to United Automobile Services from whom it was acquired by East Yorkshire in 1980. Resting opposite York railway station on 2 February 1984, it was on that occasion operating on the Hull - York service. (K.A.Jenkinson)*

*Willowbrook-bodied Leyland Leopard 206 in NBC's striped National Express livery rests at York railway station in 1986 before returning to Hull on the 746 service. (K.A.Jenkinson)*

Anlaby Common workshops just before the turn of the year. Although its roof and upper deck window pillars were removed completely, the roofless front bulkhead was retained to act as a shield against the wind. When completed, this bus (900) was painted in a striking livery of white with horizontal blue and purple stripes and was given the name 'Belvedere Star'. Sister bus 901 entered the company's workshops for similar conversion in the early spring of 1979, emerging some weeks later in a blue livery with an orange front and side panels which formed a sun whose rays pointed from it for the length of the bus and was named 'Sewerby Star'. Both buses carried the legend 'East Yorkshire Coaster' on each side below their lower deck windows and entered service at Bridlington at the start of the 1979 summer season. These bright new colour schemes were the winning designs submitted by local pupils in a competition organised by the company.

New arrivals in 1979 comprised 17 full-height ECW-bodied Bristol VRTs, again fitted with Leyland engines, 3 B-series Leyland Nationals and 6 Plaxton-bodied Leyland Leopard coaches which together replaced several older members of the fleet including the last of the Leyland panther Cubs abd AEC Renowns of which two of the latter were retained for conversion into permanent driver training vehicles. Another departure from the fleet was ex.United Plaxton-bodied Leopard coach 160 which was destroyed by fire in August and was subsequently sold for scrap.

*Wearing an all-over advertising livery incorporating a massive NBC 'double-N' logo to promote East Yorkshire's coaching activities was Bristol VRT 527, seen here on the forecourt of Anlaby Road depot, Hull. (EYMS)*

Although 8 Leyland National 2s were ordered for delivery in 1980, only seven were received, the eighth being diverted to Northern General Transport Co. These were 49-seaters and the first to arrive in January was by coincidence the first National 2 to be built apart from the prototypes. Also added to the fleet in August/September 1980 were 9 new low-height ECW-bodied Bristol VRTs which were this time powered by Gardner engines, whilst in April/May a pair of Plaxton-bodied 57-seat Leyland Leopard coaches was acquired from United Automobile Services. The first 12m vehicles in the fleet, these dated from 1971 and had started life with Samuelsons New Transport Co. Ltd. of London before passing to National Travel South East in January 1974 and United in May 1978.

Ordered for delivery in 1981 were 3 Leopard coaches, 3 Leyland National 2s, 5 Bristol VRTs and a Leyland Olympian, although as will be seen, the vehicles which actually arrived differed considerably from these. The Leopard coaches materialised with 2 carrying Willowbrook coachwork, the other being bodied by Duple, while 8 instead of 5 Bristol

VRTs arrived, 2 of which (526/7) were diverted from a Yorkshire Traction order in exchange for the 3 Leyland National 2s being built for East Yorkshire. The Olympian, which would have been the first vehicle of this type to be operated by the company was instead diverted to West Yorkshire Road Car Co. Ltd. as was the solitary Olympian ordered for delivery in 1982. In the event, neither of these two buses took their place in the West Yorkshire fleet until January 1983 ! Also obtained by East Yorkshire was a pair of secondhand eleven-year-old Duple-bodied Leopard coaches acquired from Southdown Motor Services whilst on the other side of the coin, Park Royal-bodied Daimler Fleetline 871 was unfortunately damaged in an accident in April and as a result was withdrawn from service.

The most radical change in East Yorkshire's operations for many years was made on 17 May 1981 when the co-ordination scheme between the company and Hull Corporation was superceded by a new operating agreement. The new arrangement differed in as much as both operators were allowed to keep the monies earned by their buses rather than pooling these and subsequently sharing them in a pre-determined ratio. As far as the travelling public were concerned, the city bus network which was an amalgamation of City Transport and East Yorkshire routes financially supported by Hull City Council and now identified by service numbers in the series 1 - 99 still allowed concessionary pass holders to travel on both operators' vehicles within the city boundary at the appropriate charge. On these services the City Council formulated the fares policy whereas on all other East Yorkshire routes passing through the city (numbered 100 and above), these passes were not accepted. A month later, on 7 June, East Yorkshire renumbered a large number

of their services on a zonal basis.

Another major change taking place in 1981 occurred in August when Lincolnshire Road Car Co. Ltd., who had been badly hit by the recession and service subsidy cuts, were placed under joint management with East Yorkshire. Both companies were however to remain independent of each other operationally and fleet wise and visually little change was witnessed, although a few Lincolnshire vehicles started to appear at East Yorkshire's Anlaby Common workshops for maintenance or repair.

Upon the opening of the long-awaited new Humber Bridge from Hessle to Barton upon Humber on 24 June 1981, East Yorkshire inaugurated a new limited stop service from Hull to Scunthorpe, jointly with Lincolnshire Road Car Co. Ltd. At first, Bristol VRT double deckers were the regular performers

by both companies and although the first service journey across the bridge was operated by East Yorkshire 518, two days earlier 987 had become the first bus to cross the span when it did so for trial purposes. When the Humber Bridge was 'officially' opened by Her Majesty, the Queen some months later, East Yorkshire were contracted to provide five coaches to transport the other dignitaries and guests.

A return to the past was made in November 1981 when Bristol VRT 519 was repainted into the company's original indigo blue & primrose livery for promotional purposes. Lettered 'EYMS Serving the East Riding and Humberside since 1926', and looking superb in its new 'old' colour scheme it spent much of the following year operating the company's important trunk route between Hull and Scarborough and surprisingly has retained this livery ever since. Several other of the company's buses had by this time received all-over or part-advertising liveries, thus providing a little light relief from NBC's monotonous corporate poppy red colour.

Earler in the year, on Sunday 15 March a recasting of the services between Leeds and the East Coast operated by West Yorkshire and East Yorkshire resulted in the extension through to Leeds of the latter's 746 Hull - York route curtailed between York and Leeds on 23 May 1976. The 746 was now re-routed in Tadcaster to run via Woodlands Estate instead of Station Road and at this same time, the 745 service from Bridlington to Leeds via Stamford Bridge, which consisted of two return journeys per day, was discontinued.

Although a small number of older vehicles were withdrawn and sold during 1982, including a trio of 1974 Bristol VRTs which, in August/September were sold to Lincolnshire Road Car Co.Ltd., no new buses or coaches were taken into stock. Also crossing the Humber to join Lincolnshire Road Car, albeit on short term loans during July and August were 3 Park Royal-bodied Daimler Fleetlines and a Willowbrook-bodied dual purpose Leyland Leopard whilst at this same time a Park Royal-bodied Fleetline was also loaned to South Wales Transport at Swansea. For reasons unknown, this never operated in the Principality however and spent its period of loan in store in one of South Wales' depots.

Further service cuts were implemented during the early summer of 1982 in an attempt to reduce the expected financial losses for the year, with both rural and urban operations being affected and the Saturdays only route between Grindale and Bridlington was withdrawn completely. Despite fares increases and an estimated saving of around £130,000 as a result of the cuts, the company still believed that their loss on the year would be in excess of £900,000 and announced that only substantial revenue support from Humberside County Council would prevent even more pruning taking place. On a brighter note, the 'Breakaway

Express summer routes, mainly from Hull to North and South Humberside coastal resorts, successfully launched during the previous year were reintroduced on Sundays starting in May. As the company's contribution to Maritime England Year, these special services were named 'Maritime Breakaways' and the 121 from Hull to Scarborough was also added to this list.

Although no new vehicles joined the fleet during 1982, a secondhand purchase was made in the form of a 1961 vintage MCCW-bodied convertible open top Leyland Atlantean formerly operated in Western National's Devon General fleet. Numbered 902 by its new owner, it was placed in service on Bridlington's sea-front service still in the ivory and red colours in which it had been received, apart from the addition of a red waistband, and was given the name 'Flamborough Star'

Just as 1982 had been a comparatively quiet year on the vehicle front, in contrast 1983 proved to be a year of activity with comings and goings almost every month. The first Leyland Tigers to join the East Yorkshire fleet made their debut in March when a pair of Plaxton high-floor coach-bodied examples took up their duties. Two more arrived in June, with a further pair following in August (all standard height 'express' examples) although it was January 1984 before one of the latter eventually entered service. March also witnessed the arrival of the company's first Leyland Olympians, these carrying ECW bus-type bodywork of 13ft. 8in. height. Surprisingly, only one of these was immediately licensed for use, the other remaining in store until 1 October before making its debut in revenue-earning service. As a result, this had to be re-registered from its original GRH529Y mark to A529MAT. Completing the year's delivery of new vehicles were 3 ECW-bodied, coach-seated Olympians which arrived in December wearing an all-white livery. These were immediately placed in store and did not enter service until May/June 1984, by which time they had gained indigo stripes in the by now standard NBC 'dual purpose' style to their previously plain livery.

Three more convertible open-top MCCW-bodied PDR1/1 Atlanteans were acquired from Western National during 1983, the first of which arrived in February in time to be painted white with black stripes (the colours of Hull R.F.C., one of the two local rugby league teams) before entering service st Bridlington at the start of the summer season. Named 'Bridlington Star', this was given fleet number 903. The other two did not arrive until September/October and were placed in store for the duration of the winter without being used. Another secondhand vehicle to be acquired came in June in the form of an ECW-bodied Bristol RELL6G. Purchased from Lincolnshire Road Car Co., this was obtained for conversion into a mobile travel office, a task

*Former Western National (Devon General) converible open-top MCCW-bodied Leyland Atlantean 902 (926GTA) has its top removed at Bridlington depot in preparation for the summer season in 1984. (EYMS)*

*ECW-bodied Bristol RELL6G LFE832H was acquired from Lincolnshire Road Car Co.Ltd. in 1983 for conversion to a mobile office. Painted in all-over white livery, it is seen here shortly after taking up its new duties. (EYMS)*

*The first Leyland Olympian to join the East Yorkshire fleet was ECW-bodied 528 which is seen in NBC poppy red & white livery at Rougier Street, York on the 746 service from Hull to Leeds in April 1983. (K.A.Jenkinson)*

*Acquired in 1983 from Western National, 903 (931GTA) was a Leyland Atlantean with MCCW convertible open-top bodywork. Seen at Bridlington with its top removed, it was named 'Bridlington Star' and was painted in a white & black livery. (T.W.W.Knowles)*

undertaken by a Cottingham coachbuilder and completed in January 1984.

Unusually, two of the ex.Western National convertible open-top Atlanteans, after the summer season at Bridlington ended, were transferred to Hull, after having their tops replaced, they were placed in service during September on a variety of duties. The year also saw the almost complete closure of the company's central workshops at Anlaby Common - closed save for a lone fuel pump engineer who was the only occupant for several months until the works were reopened to cater for the additional engineering work anticipated with the bringing of Lincolnshire Road Car Co. Ltd. under common control.

In order to overcome a vehicle shortage caused by the gaining of a number of new contracts in the Hull area, the company hired five vehicles in July, four of which came from East Midland Motor Services Ltd. Of these, two were ECW-bodied Bristol VRTs, the other two being Alexander-bodied Daimler Fleetlines and in the event, the latter pair were never used by their adopted owner, remaining instead in store at Anlaby Road depot from their arrival on 6 July until their return home a week later. The VRTs, still in their

owner's NBC leaf green & white livery were given East Yorkshire fleet names and were operated on duties in Hull from 4 July until 26 July when they too returned home. The fifth vehicle hired was however much more unusual. A Leyland-DAB articulated single decker originally used in

*One of a pair of MCCW convertible open-top bodied Leyland Atlanteans acquired from Western National (Devon General) in 1983, 904 (932GTA) is seen outside Anlaby Road, Hull depot after having its top refitted for use during the winter months. (EYMS)*

Sheffield by South Yorkshire PTE, this was hired from Leyland Vehicles Ltd. from 12 July until 2 September.

On the other side of the coin, withdrawn Duple Dominant bus-bodied Ford 171 was put to use as a waiting room at Ferensway Coach Station, Hull soon after the start of the year and on 11 January, withdrawn Park Royal-bodied Fleetline 868 was loaned to Lincolnshire Road Car Co. with whom it remained until 3 March. Following it across the Humber early in April were the two ex.Southdown Duple-bodied Leyland Leopard coaches 209/10 which were loaned to Lincolnshire for the summer season, returning home on 26 October when they were placed in store for disposal.

Finally, before the year ended, Leyland National 169 was taken into Anlaby Common workshops for modifications to make it suitable for use by the disabled. This involved providing a wheelchair ramp at the entrance and the fitting of coach-style seating. Appearing in its new guise in October painted in NBC-style poppy red & white 'local coach' livery, it could be used as either a 49-seater or as a 25-seater plus 8 wheelchairs.

1984 opened with the appearance of Marshall-bodied Leyland Panther 848 as a mobile training room. This had been an on-off project started in July 1982, and after being threatened with abandonment several times, it was somewhat surprising that it was eventually completed. As a result of its pending sale along with its four sisters, Duple Dominant bus-bodied Ford 171 was replaced as a waiting

room at Ferensway Coach Station, Hull by ex.Shaw Bros./United Plaxton-bodied Leyland Leopard 241 in January, the five Fords eventually being sold to NBC's disposal concern at Bracebridge Heath, Lincoln for export to Perth, Australia. Another vehicle relegated to non-passenger carrying duties was open-top Atlantean 901 which in January was put to use as a staff mess room at Bridlington depot.

February saw the arrival of a luxurious Roe Doyen-bodied Leyland Royal Tiger coach which, with seating for 50 passengers was regarded as the new flagship of the fleet. Two more coaches of this type were received in August and these proved to be the company's only new vehicles in 1984. Whilst the first of these was away for modifications during July, Leyland Vehicles loaned the company a brand-new Royal Tiger-Doyen demonstrator which spent two weeks with East Yorkshire.

One of the ex.Western National convertible open-top Atlanteans, 905, which had remained in store since its purchase in October 1983 was sold to Lincolnshire Road Car Co. Ltd. in February in exchange for an identical bus which was acquired by East Yorkshire solely for spares. 905's

*Disaster struck on 13 January 1984 when the company's depot at Beverley was completely destroyed by severe gales. Several vehicle sustained damage whilst a Bristol RELL of Lincolnshire Road Car Co. which was in store (and can be seen amongst the debris) was completely destroyed. (EYMS)*

sister (904) which had also been in store since its arrival in September 1985 was in February repainted white with two-tone blue bands in NBC style similar to the 1983 Olympians and named 'Belvedere Star' for use at Bridlington during the summer season. Surprisingly however, 904 was placed in service in March with its roof re-fitted and did not operate in its intended form until June.

Disaster struck at Beverley on 13 January when during the severe gales, the roof of the depot caved in. This badlt damaged a couple of employees' cars and completed the demolition of Lincolnshire Road Car. Co. Bristol RELL 1215 which was stored there having already been damaged by fire. The wreckage of the garage roof also closed the adjacent railway line for a time, and ironically, East Yorkshire were called upon to provide a rail replacement service. So great was the damage, that what remained of the depot had to be demolished later in the month with the result that the small allocation of buses based at that town had thereafter to be parked in the bus station at Sow Hill. Later in the year, in August, the bus station at Bridlington was vacated and sold to the Borough Council for redevelopment, the services using it being moved to pick up and set down their passengers in a nearby street. For the remainder of the holiday season - and indeed ever since - the former bus station was then used by the local authority as a 'temporary' car park.

Further departures across the river took place when B-series Leyland National 181 was sold to Lincolnshire in April. Two months later, a Plaxton-bodied Leopard coach and a 49-seat Leyland National were despatched to Lincolnshire on loan and whilst the Leopard returned to Hull on 2 July, the

National remained in South Humberside and was eventually purchased by Lincolnshire in October along with two more of East Yorkshire's buses of this type. Despite having been withdrawn for disposal in 1983 following their return from Lincolnshire Road Car Co., the two ex.Southdown Leopard coaches were both reinstated at Hull in July 1984 to give a few more weeks service.

In a bid to encourage more people to avail themselves of their bus services etc., East Yorkshire on 9 October began to sell their Explorer and weekly/4 weekly Saver tickets through 205 Post Offices throughout North Humberside, this innovation proving successful in gaining more passengers in the months and years ahead.

Following the resignation as General Manager of East Yorkshire and Lincolnshire Road Car Co. on 31 December 1984 of Stuart Senior who was to take up the appointment of General Manager of United Automobile Services Ltd., his former position was filled by Alan Stephenson who, since 1977 had been Company Secretary of West Yorkshire Road Car Co.Ltd. Although his arrival brought few changes at first, he was eventually to bring the company into a new age, as will be seen later.

*Plaxton Paramount 3200-bodied Leyland Tiger 6 (A!06MKH) is seen here when new painted in NBC's corporate all-white National coaching livery. (EYMS)*

*Carlyle-converted Ford Transit 301 was numerically the first minibus purchased new by East Yorkshire. Making its debut in 1986 it wore a new livery of silver with blue & red stripes and a black skirt and carried 'Little Bus' fleet names. (EYMS)*

*One of East Yorkshire's 1985 batch of Leyland Olympians, coach-seated 533 shows off its white & two-tone blue livery as it rests at Hull's Ferensway bus park on 16 April 1990 before taking up its duties on the 121 service to Scarborough. (J.Whitmore)*

1985 began with the arrival of three more coach-seated ECW-bodied Leyland Olympians which, in January took up their duties on the company's longer distance services in their predominantly white livery. These were followed in March by a pair of new Plaxton-bodied Leyland Tiger coaches, one of which was painted in National Holidays livery and in May, two of the 1983 Plaxton-bodied Tigers were fitted with onboard toilets to make them suitable for use on National Express operations requiring this facility. Meanwhile, between February and April several of East Yorkshire's older Leopard coaches had their registration numbers replaced with 'cherished' dateless numbers, one of which had been transferred from the company's AEC Bridgemaster tree lopper, the others having been purchased specially for this purpose.

In preparation for the reorganisation of some of Bridlington's town services, the company ordered their first minibuses, seven Ford Transits with van-derived Dormobile 16-seat bodies converted by Carlyle. The first of these arrived in August and was joined by the remaining six early the next month. Painted in a livery of silver-grey with one red and one mid-blue stripe, these new additions to the fleet carried the fleet name 'East Yorkshire Little Bus'. On 27 September, six of the Transits took up their duties in Bridlington on two new town services which operated on a hail-and-ride basis, picking up and setting down passengers anywhere enroute outside the town centre, the seventh being used on a similar duty at Hornsea starting on the following day. As a result of the success of this new type of vehicle,

the company ordered a further six for use in other areas.

Prior to this, East Yorkshire's coaching fleet had been expanded by the acquisition in October from Yorkshire Traction of a pair of Plaxton-bodied Leyland Tigers equipped to National Express Rapide standards and painted in that livery. Arriving on cherished number plates which had to be returned to Yorkshire Traction, these two coaches were given new dateless registration marks by their new owner before the end of the year.

The final additions to the fleet made their appearance in December in the form of 2 Leyland Doyen-bodied Royal Tiger coaches of executive standard. Fitted with an onboard toilet, servery, video and cellnet radio telephone, both could be used as conventional 46-seaters or with 39 seats and 6 tables. Painted in a striking silver livery with indigo and riviera blue stripes, these carried the lettering 'East Yorkshire Diplomat' to further signify their luxury status.

Following the announcement under the 1985 Transport Act that all NBC's subsidiaries had to be privatised before 1988, East Yorkshire along with several other NBC companies decided to break away from the corporate colour scheme

*Looking immaculate in its 'East Yorkshire Diplomat' livery as its stands on the forecourt of Anlaby Road depot, Hull, Leyland Royal Tiger Doyen 16 which carries cherished registration number 794EYD (East Yorkshire Dipolmat) was originally registered C116DRH. (P.J.S.Shipp)*

which had been forced upon them some eleven years earlier and in the late autumn began to experiment with new livery layouts. The first bus to show these outward-signs of change was Bristol VRT 987 which gained white lower deck window frames to its otherwise standard NBC poppy red livery. This was quickly followed by another VRT, 974, which in addition to receiving white lower deck window surrounds, also gained a white roof. Completing the experimental trio was Bristol VRT 980 which appeared in NBC poppy red with white between-decks panels.

In what was to be its final year before de-regulation, East Yorkshire's fleet numbered 176 buses and coaches, of which 9 were delicensed or withdrawn for disposal. These were allocated 90 to Anlaby Road, Hull; 25 to Bridlington; 21 to Driffield/Hornsea; 7 each to Elloughton and Pocklington and 14 to Withernsea. A further 3 were licensed but retained in reserve.

The introduction of the deregulation of local bus services on 26 October 1986 caused the company to spend many months earlier in the year examining their services, deciding which of these warranted commercial registration and calculating tenders to be submitted for subsidised routes. Although a few operations were lost in the process and the prospect of challenges by independent and other operators loomed on the horizon, East Yorkshire were confident of their future and indeed gained a substantial number of additional contracts in the Hull area. Placing even more pressure on the company's already well-burdened management was the expansion of the company's territory in September. In its preparations for privatisation, the NBC had decided that some of its larger subsidiaries should be sub divided into smaller units, and amongst these was United Automobile Services whose northern-most part was to be divested in a new company, Northumbria Motor Services Ltd., and its operations in the area to the south of Whitby transferred to East Yorkshire Motor Services Ltd. Although it was decreed that this was to take place on 1 September 1986, the actual transfer of interests to East Yorkshire was effected on 8 September when Pickering and Scarborough depots, their operations and 70 vehicles were placed under the Hull-based company's control. The vehicles concerned comprised 23 Bristol VRTs; 4 Leyland Olympians; 14 Leyland Leopards; 7 Leyland Tigers; 3 Leyland Nationals; 1 Bristol RELL; 1 Bristol RESL; 1 Bristol RELH; 2 Bristol LHs and 14 Mercedes Benz L608D minibuses. Those operating from Pickering and Scarborough depots were all given 'Scarborough & District' fleet names and the minibuses continued to operate under their existing Scarborough Skipper identity. Deregulation on 26 October had also meant the end of the long-standing co-ordination (later operating) agreement with Hull City Council since such agreements were outlawed under rules of the new Transport Act.

Prior to the addition of the above vehicles, East Yorkshire's fleet had been updated by the arrival of 13 new vehicles between February and June, the first of which were 6 Ford Transit minibuses with Carlyle 18-seat bodywork. These were obtained for use on new services planned to start on 24 March in Bridlington where the 'Little Buses' had been hailed as a success and additionally in Beverley on 14 April and in the Willerby and Anlaby areas adjacent to Hull. In April, a trio of 79-seat MCW Metroliner double deck coaches were received, although one of these, having not been used by East Yorkshire was almost immediately despatched to Wessex of Bristol in exchange for 2 new Duple 340-bodied Leyland Tiger coaches diverted from that company. A month earlier another 3 coach-seated ECW-bodied Olympians were received and added to these were 4 secondhand Park Royal-bodied single-door Leyland Atlanteans purchased from Northern General Transport Co. in May/June.

Finding themselves with insufficient vehicles with which to operate the large number of new contracts gained which were to commence in September, the company embarked upon a search for secondhand buses that were immediately available. This led to the arrival of no fewer than 36 vehicles between July and September, all but 4 of which were double deckers. The main source of supply was Northern General Transport from whom 6 ECW-bodied dual door Leyland Atlantean AN68s, 2 ECW-bodied Bristol VRTs, 11 Park Royal-bodied AN68s, 2 Atlantean PDR1/1s and 3 Leyland Nationals were obtained. Of these, the Park Royal-bodied AN68s and PDR1s were unusual in that they had been converted to open top configuration by Northern General in 1986 for export to Saudi Arabia, but following the cancellation of this order had been placed in store where they remained until their sale to East Yorkshire. Their conversion involved only the removal of the between-domes

*Above : United's Scarborough-based fleet contained a number of Reeve Burgess-bodied 20-seat Mercedes Benz L608D minibuses which were painted in 'Skipper' livery. One of these - 411 - circumnavigates the traffic island near the resort's railway station after its transfer to the newly-created Scarborough & District fleet. (K.A.Jenkinson)*

*Left : Still painted in United's poppy red & white livery but having gained Scarborough & District's original-style fleet name vinyls is 725 (BPT925S), one of the company's inherited ECW-bodied Bristol VRTs. (P.J.S.Shipp)*

section of the roof, leaving the side windows in their original form. Completing the 36 vehicles taken into stock were 5 Park Royal-bodied Leyland Atlantean AN68s originating from Greater Manchester PTE and 6 ECW-bodied Bristol VRTs and a Leyland National from Devon General. With the exception of the open-top Atlanteans, all of which were temporarily placed in store by their new owner, the remainder of the new acquisitions entered service almost immediately and whilst the majority were first painted into East Yorkshire's new red & white livery, 5 of the Devon General VRTs made their debut still in their former owner's colours, one still being in the old NBC leaf green & white hue - complete with East Yorkshire fleet names.

Earlier in the year, the livery experiments had continued with a pair of Bristol VRTs appearing in dark red with white lower deck window frames and Park Royal-bodied Atlantean 957 being repainted dark red with an NBC-style white centre band. In November, Plaxton-bodied Leopard 190 which, along with another of the company's coaches had been given a 'cherished' registration number during the summer, was given East Yorkshire's old coaching livery of primrose and riviera blue and named 'Holderness Star' as a reminder of a former era.

The need for an additional minibus for use at Beverley led to the hiring of a Carlyle-bodied Ford Transit from West Yorkshire Road Car Co. Ltd. from the beginning of May whilst during August a Robin Hood-bodied Fiat Daily 79.10 minibus was borrowed for evaluation at Bridlington. Other strangers to the company came from Greater Manchester Buses who, from 27 October until March 1987 loaned a coach (usually a Duple-bodied Leyland Tiger) to East Yorkshire for use on their Trans-Pennine National Express service from Hull to Liverpool. This followed major damage to Duple-bodied Leopard 208 received in an accident while in the care of a Greater Manchester driver. The 'loaned' coach was changed periodically to allow its return to its rightful owner for routine maintenance etc. Following the transfer of

United Automobile Services' Scarborough operations to East Yorkshire, one of the 'acquired' Olympians (539) which had been received wearing an all-over advertising livery was, as a result of this, in September despatched to United for operation in darlington and its surrounds. In exchange, East

*Parked outside Anlaby Road depot, Hull soon after their acquisition by East Yorkshire in 1986 are a trio of ex.Devon General Bristol VRTs. ATA554L and ATL563L still carry their previous owner's poppy red livery and fleet names while ATA557L was painted NBC leaf green. (P.J.S.Shipp)*

*East Yorkshire's former Northern General ECW-bodied Bristol VRT 924 - with its centre door sealed and minus fleet names - stands alongside Leyland Olympian 528 at Ferensway bus park, Hull in 1987 still wearing NBC-style poppy red livery. (M.Wells)*

Yorkshire received a United Olympian for several weeks, this being changed for a United Bristol VRT in November when 539 moved from Darlington to Middlesborough. Its return home, and the departure of United's VRT took place in December.

In the meantime, one of the ECW-bodied Atlanteans acquired from Northern General was converted from dual to single door by the permanent sealing of its centre exit and a start was made on the refitting of roofs to some of the ex.Northern General open-top Atlanteans, the first of which made its debut on North Humberside in January 1987. Some of this work was contracted out to Kirkby Central (dealers) at Anston whilst others were dealt with in the company's own workshops at Anlaby Common.

The first new vehicles to be purchased in 1987 arrived in January in the form of 5 Robin Hood-bodied 16-seat Iveco 49.10s with coach-type seating. These were finished in a blue livery similar to the two 'Diplomat' Doyens and began to enter service in March.

Despite the deregulation of local bus services having now taken place, the feared competition from independent operators had not materialised and except for competition from Hedon Coaches' infrequent service between Hedon and Hull and Appleby's and Hornsby's Sunday operation of the cross-river 350 Humberlink service, East Yorkshire faced no other challengers. Services in the Hull area remained virtually unchanged except for some increased frequencies and it seemed as if the peaceful situation would remain for some time to come. Similarly the company found that its other main operating areas such as Scarborough, Bridlington and Beverley remained largely unchallenged, although this was set to change before a further year elapsed.

*One of eight Park Royal-bodied Leyland Atlanteans acquired from Greater Manchester PTE in 1986 to assist East Yorkshire following deregulation, 913 rests at Ferensway bus park, Hull between its duties on the 47 service to Willerby. (T.W.W.Knowles)*

# RETURNED TO PRIVATE OWNERSHIP

Undoubtedly, the news of the year was East Yorkshire's privatisation from the National Bus Company which took place on 3 February following a successful bid by the company's senior management headed by managing director Alan Stephenson and supported by commercial manager Peter Shipp, financial director Godfrey Burley, and four other senior managers. This buy-out was achieved by the formation of a holding company, EYMS Ltd, later to become EYMS Group Ltd., which was owned by the management team and acquired all the shares in the original East Yorkshire company, this becoming a wholly-owned subsidiary. Subsequent acquisitions were all bought by this holding company rather than by East Yorkshire Motor Services Ltd., as often erroneously reported in the press. Thus, after almost twenty years under state control, East Yorkshire was now once again free to pursue its own plans and formulate its own policies and decisions and within a matter of weeks, the first stage of the company's future expansion was set in motion. This led to the acquisition on 13 April of the business and operations of Cherry Coaches of Anlaby, providing the company with several additional stage carriage and contract services and a further 19 buses and coaches.

Originating in Beverley in the years before World War I, Percy William Cherry originally built 'Owd Bob' bicycles and later, in 1932 started a bus service in his home town using a 13-seat Morris Commercial. Expansion was slow and the fleet never grew beyond one vehicle until 1948 when a second town service was inaugurated in Beverley. Since that date, several more services have been operated around the Yorkshire Wolds and the fleet size increased. Both new and secondhand vehicles were purchased and coaching activities were embarked upon. R.P.Cherry joined his father in the business and persuaded him to acquire a secondhand double decker for contract use and this looked very distinctive in the company's black & cream livery. Taking over the Newport to Goole service of Holt, Newport, Cherry Coaches also secured several lucrative contracts to and from the British Aerospace factory at Brough and in 1986, although retaining their premises in Beverley, moved their headquarters to Springfield Way, Anlaby. At the time of their sale to East Yorkshire, their fleet comprised 2 Leyland Atlanteans; 4 Leyland Leopards; 5 Ford R1114s; 4 Volvo B58s and a Ford R1014 plus a trio of withdrawn vehicles.

Rather than absorb the Cherry operations into their own,

*Plaxton-bodied Ford R1114 YKG822T was acquired by the EYMS Group in 1987 with the Cherry fleet which it had joined a few months earlier from Bruce, Pitscottie. It is seen here in Cherry's cream & black livery at the company's Anlaby depot. (P.J.S.Shipp)*

East Yorkshire decided to retain their newly-acquired business as a subsidiary under the title of 'Cherry Coaches Ltd' although the registered office was moved to the company's headquarters at 252 Anlaby Road, Hull. Both the

*Leyland National 168 (PCN423M) seen here at Ferensway bus park, Hull wearing an all-red livery was acquired from Northern General in 1986. (T.W.W.Knowles)*

*Collecting its passengers in Bridlington whilst operating a National Holidays feeder service is Scarborough & District's appropriately-liveried ex. United Plaxton Paramount 3500-bodied Leyland Tiger 35 which, when caught by the camera in June 1987, still additionally carried its previous operator's fleet number (1035) above its driver's offside window. (K.A.Jenkinson)*

*39, a coach-seated Robin Hood-bodied Iveco 49.10 was one of a number of vehicles to carry 'East Yorkshire Bridlington' fleet names for a period of time. It is seen here in that coastal town in July 1988. (K.A.Jenkinson)*

*Wearing East Yorkshire's attractive white & two-tone blue livery and carrying 'Bridlington' lettering above its front wheel arch is Plaxton Paramount-bodied Volvo B10M 47 (B902SPR). Acquired from Excelsior Holidays, Bournemouth in 1987 it is seen here at Bridlington depot in July 1988. (K.A.Jenkinson)'*

Anlaby and Beverley depots remained in use and at first there was little sign of any change of ownership. On 25 July however, Cherry's Beverley town services were replaced by a modified minibus network and their depot at Morleys Yard, Beverley was no longer used, East Yorkshire having now transferred their operations to part of the former railway goods yard in Mill Lane.

Meanwhile, East Yorkshire had added several more vehicles to their fleet having purchased new a Duple 320-bodied Leyland Tiger and a pair of Duple 340-bodied Volvo B10M coaches, one of which was painted in 'Diplomat' livery for use at Scarborough. A total of 5 more new Iveco 49.10 minis were bought, these having Robin Hood dual purpose 19-seat bodies painted in 'Little Bus' colours whilst obtained from Yeates (dealers) of Loughborough in April was a Plaxton-bodied Volvo B10M formerly operated by Excelsior Holidays, Bournemouth. A surprise departure from the company's previous policy was the ordering of 3 Ford Sierra diesel taxis for services based on Scarborough and Hornsea although in the event these were never used in their intended role and were sold after only a short period of time. On the other side of the coin, a withdrawn Bristol VRT and a Leyland Leopard coach which had suffered fire damage following an arson attack while parked outside the back of Withernsea garage, had their bodies removed by W.Norths (dealers) of Sherburn in Elmet in March after which their chassis were

*Happily, incidents such as the fire which destroyed all-over advertising liveried ECW-bodied Bristol VRT 521 are rare occurrences. (P.J.S.Shipp)*

*Its operational days ended, Park Royal-bodied Leyland Atlantean 866 donated its front roof dome to one of its sisters before finally being sold for scrap. (P.J.S.Shipp)*

Inherited by Scarborough & District from United with their Scarborough operations in 1986 was open-top Bristol VRT 655 (YHN655M). Painted in an all-over advertising livery, it passes the resort's Harbour while working the sea-front service on 10 August 1988.    (K.A.Jenkinson)

One of five former Trent Alexander-bodied Leyland Leopards inherited from United in 1986, Scarborough & District 114 (PRR14R) leaves Valley Bridge bus station, Scarborough at the start of its journey to Pickering on a wet July day in 1988. (K.A.Jenkinson)

returned and placed in store at Pocklington depot. Although it was intended that these should be rebodied as part of a pilot scheme designed to extend the lives of several older vehicles of these types, this was never proceeded with and after remaining in limbo at Pocklington for twelve months, both were eventually cut up for scrap.

During April, East Yorkshire discontinued the use of fare boxes on their buses operating in the Hull area, reverting to normal ticket machines and once again giving passengers change instead of expecting them to tender the exact fare. This move was greatly welcomed by the travelling public who had never really accepted the fare box scheme since its inception several years earlier. During the following month, in an attempt to stem the losses being suffered in the Bridlington area, the company transferred the operation of their trunk service 121 (Hull - Bridlington - Scarborough) from Bridlington to Driffield depot, this resulting in a minor reduction of the fleet strength at Bridlington.

Strangers to North Humberside were a trio of Plaxton coach-bodied Bristol RELH6Ls hired from Lincolnshire Road Car Co. Ltd. early in June. Of these, 2 were at first used by Cherry Coaches whilst the third was operated by East Yorkshire although after a couple of weeks, one of the Cherry pair moved to East Yorkshire with whom it remained

until the end of the month when all three were returned to their rightful owner. Two of the semi-open-top ex.Northern General Atlanteans eventually entered service in this form at the beginning of the summer season on Scarborough's sea-front service, although prior to doing so, both were converted from dual to single door configuration.

Still finding themselves short of double deckers, East Yorkshire purchased three more Park Royal-bodied Atlanteans from Greater Manchester Buses in July whilst two of their Olympians had their stage carriage seats replaced with coach-type seats by Optare, Leeds in July and were repainted into their owner's white and blue dual purpose livery.

Seeking further expansion, East Yorkshire on 1 September surprisingly purchased a taxi firm in Hull operating under the title Pheonix Radio Taxis. Formed by R.A.Trebilcock, Pheonix Radio Taxis operated a fleet of over 20 cars in addition to a Reeve Burgess-bodied 12-seat Mercedes L307D minicoach and 3 Volkswagen Transporters on taxi plates. Registered as Pheonix Radio Taxis Ltd., this new company operated as a separate subsidiary of EYMS Ltd., its operations being based alongside the Cherry fleet at Springfield Way, Anlaby.

As one door opened, another one closed however and

In order to increase its fleet for deregulation in 1986, East Yorkshire purchased a quantity of secondhand double deckers including a number from Northern General. Two of these, ECW dual-door bodied Leyland Atlantean 910 (MPT310P) and Park Royal-bodied 905 (RCN112N) are seen here at Ferensway bus park, Hull in April 1989. (K.A.Jenkinson)

following severe financial losses suffered in the Bridlington area, partly due to the loss of six school contracts and partly due to the poor summer weather, major service cuts were implemented on 5 September at the end of the summer season. Although the 'Little Buses' operations were not affected, the only conventional services to remain unchanged were those running between Bridlington and Carnaby Industrial Estate. Indeed, the 3 and 3A services to Flamborough were axed completely and most others were given a reduced frequency.

However, not letting this stand in the way of their plans for further expansion, East Yorkshire purchased the Scarborough operations of Wallace Arnold of Leeds together with its Hardwick's Services Ltd. subsidiary on 5 October thus further consolidating the company's position in that seaside town. In addition to adding a further 18 vehicles to their fleet, it also gave them two more depots in Scarborough, some valuable town centre property, a kiosk at West Pier and a depot at Snainton.

D.Hardwick of Snainton, a few miles outside Scarborough had begun bus operation during the 'twenties when he began a service from his home village to the coastal resort primarily for the benefit of shoppers. Later expanding into the field of coaching, and gaining several local contracts to schools and factories, Hardwick later took over the business of Willings & Noble of Scarborough who traded under the title of Forge Valley Coaches and gradually expanded his fleet to some 14 buses and coaches, most of which had been purchased new.In March 1952, Hardwick sold his business, operations and premises to Wallace Arnold Tours of Leeds who continued to operate the business as a subsidiary and during the following year introduced double deckers to the fleet. Operation of this type of vehicle continued until 1971 when the last example, a Roe-bodied Leyland PD3, was withdrawn and the single deck once again dominated. Wallace Arnold had meanwhile expanded their coaching operations in Scarborough from their depot in Columbus Ravine and employed their fleet on a wide selection of excursions during the busy summer months, adding to these a lucrative contract to transport workers to and from the RCA establishment at Fylingdales on the North Yorkshire Moors. A special fleet of older coaches was maintained for the latter purpose, these having been downgraded from their previous coaching activities.

East Yorkshire's acquisition of Wallace Arnold's Scarborough activities and those of Hardwick's added 11 Plaxton-bodied Leopards; 2 Leyland Nationals; 2 Reeve Burgess 19-seat Mercedes L508D minicoaches and a Caetano-bodied Fiat 79.14 19-seat coach to their fleet together with a pair of open-top Atlanteans which had been operated in competition with Scarborough & District on the resort's sea front during the summer of 1987. Although the newly-acquired company was absorbed into East Yorkshire's

*Acquired by Wallace Arnold from Greater Manchester PTE for its subsidiary Hardwicks fleet, Leyland National WBN475T shows off its new owner's livery as it stands opposite Wallace Arnold's depot in Columbus Ravine, Scarborough. (T.Carter)*

Scarborough operations, the Hardwicks name was retained as were the depots included in the deal at Beaconsfield Street and Columbus ravine, Scarborough and at Snainton. The Hardwick fleet however was quickly to see change and during the remainder of the year, the Leopards were transferred to Scarborough & District in exchange for several Leyland Nationals, two of which were repainted in Hardwick colours and given their fleet name. In addition, a trio of Plaxton Paramount-bodied Leyland Tigers were hired from West Yorkshire Road Car Co. Ltd. (another company controlled by Alan Stephenson) for a few weeks in October/November.

The custom of transferring vehicles between East Yorkshire's various fleets was now becoming common place and in addition to those mentioned above, a pair of East Yorkshire Leyland Leopard coaches were despatched to join the Cherry operation at Anlaby in October as replacements for older members of that fleet which were then withdrawn for eventual disposal. Two secondhand coaches, one an ex.Smith Shearings Ford R1114, the other a Plaxton-bodied Leyland Tiger from Roberts, Cefn Mawr were also purchased for the Cherry fleet in October and December respectively and received that company's new livery of cream with red and black bands. A more unusual purchase was an East Lancs-bodied AEC Regent V which was acquired from a Hull dealer in exchange for AEC Renown 780 which had since May 1980 been used by East Yorkshire as a driver training

*Carrying an all-over advertising livery, Scarborough & District open-top Park Royal-bodied Leyland Atlantean 619 (WBN959L) was acquired with Wallace Arnold's Scarborough operations in 1987. New to Greater Manchester PTE, it is seen here leaving Corner Cafe, Scarborough on 6 July 1988 while working the resort's sea front service. (K.A.Jenkinson)*

*Acquired by East Yorkshire with Wallace Arnold's Scarborough operations in 1987 was C158DWT, a Caetano-bodied Fiat 79.14 which is seen here at Scarborough on 6 July 1988 still in its original owner's colours. (K.A.Jenkinson)*

*Right : Tri-axle Talbot Pullman demonstrator G133AHP was used by East Yorkshire for a period of time for evaluation purposes, although no vehicles of this type were ever purchased. It is seen here carrying 'Little Bus' fleet names and East Yorkshire legal lettering. (EYMS)*

*Below : Wearing Scarborough & District's new red & portland grey livery and fleet names, former United Bristol VRT 712 (PUF593R) stands in Valley Bridge bus station in its home town while being used on local services. (T.W.W.Knowles)*

vehicle. New to Southampton City Transport in 1965, the 'new' Regent V was immaculately painted in its new owner's traditional indigo blue & primrose livery before it took up its duties as a driver training bus in the final month of the year.

Further vehicles of the ancillary fleet to make the news were the Bristol RELL mobile office which, in December, was put to use as a waiting room at Ferensway coach station, Hull and Leyland Panther 848 which was employed as a mobile workshop at Beverley depot during the latter part of the year.

Following the popularity of minibuses in other parts of East Yorkshire's operating area, Little Buses were introduced to Cottingham and Hessle during December with one half hourly service Monday to Saturday service in the former and three hourly services on Mondays to Fridays in the latter. The Hessle routes, which were to run for a three month trial period were operated on a Community Bus basis, although unlike most similar schemes throughout Britain, the East Yorkshire drivers were not unpaid.

1988 began with the restructuring of East Yorkshire Motor Services to form the EYMS Group Ltd. This included the incorporation of Scarborough & District Motor Services Ltd. and Hardwicks Services Ltd. as separate limited companies and applications were made for 105 and 20 operating discs respectively. Scarborough & District had adopted a dark red livery with grey lower deck window frames for its 'big bus' fleet and although all the vehicles operating from Scarborough and Pickering depots carried Scarborough & District fleet names, those at Bridlington surprisingly retained East Yorkshire names, although some additionally carried 'Bridlington' above their front wheel arch. Hardwicks used East Yorkshire's corporate livery style but instead of white

and blue, used deep cream with a brown skirt and orange band at floor level. A new company under the title of Associated Bus & Coach Parts Ltd. was formed jointly with West Yorkshire Road Car Co. Ltd. to supply spares etc. to both companies whilst Kingston Management Services Ltd. was incorporated to provide accountancy, financial and legal services for the EYMS Group. A further company set up to provide the Group's engineering functions at their Anlaby Common workshops and at a new supporting workshop unit established at Bridlington depot was EYMS Group Engineering Ltd. and completing the restructuring was Travelworld (Yorkshire) Ltd. which was formed to control the Group's four ABTA travel agencies - the latest of which had been opened at Cottingham in December 1987 - and the bus and coach travel shops at Bridlington and Ferensway coach station, Hull. Alan Stephenson became chairman and managing director of EYMS Group Ltd. whilst Peter Shipp took over as managing director of East Yorkshire Motor Services Ltd., Godfrey Burley as managing director of Kingston Management Services Ltd., Gordon Jones as Group engineer, Peter Lanfranchi as manager of ABC Parts Ltd. and Margaret Briggs as general manager of Travelworld (Yorkshire) Ltd. The Group's chief accountant was Ed Hogan whilst the general manager of Scarborough & District was Eric Boyes who also had responsibility for Hardwicks.

The first additions to the fleet in 1988 arrived in January in the form of 3 Plaxton-bodied Volvo B10Ms which were purchased from a dealer. Starting life in 1985 with Capital Coaches of West Drayton, this trio entered service with their new owner in its corporate livery of white with indigo blue skirt and riviera blue band. Joining these in March were 3 new Duple 340-bodied Leyland Tigers, one of which was finished in National Express Rapide livery and 3 ECW-bodied Bristol VRTs hired from Yorkshire Traction to cover a temporary double deck shortage within the fleet.

Transfers between the Group's fleets continued at pace with buses and coaches moving between them with increased regularity as operations demanded. Amongst these was one of the ex.Northern General open-top Atlanteans which, after having its roof refitted was despatched to Cherry Coaches as a replacement for an older double decker which was then withdrawn. Having a small surplus of small capacity vehicles, two of the coach-seated Iveco 49.10 minis were loaned in February to Premier Travel of Cambridge (another of the AJS companies owned independently of EYMS by Alan Stephenson). These returned to Hull on 25 March whilst two similar vehicles were sold to AJS group company, West Yorkshire Road Car Co. Ltd. during this same month.

Following their withdrawal from National Holidays work, the remaining coaches wearing this livery were repainted into East Yorkshire's corporate colours whereas in April the three

*Unloading its passengers in Valley Bridge bus station, Scarborough in July 1988, Hardwicks' Plaxton-bodied Leyland Leopard 30 (NGR121T) originated from United with their Scarborough operations in 1986. (K.A.Jenkinson)*

Leyland Royal Tiger Doyens were surprisingly given Wallace Arnold livery which, although not featuring the 'WA' initials on their front panels, incorporated that company's fleet name on their sides. For just the one season in 1988, this trio operated Wallace Arnold holiday tours on contract to that company until all three were repainted in East Yorkshire coach colours at the end of the year. As a result of the rationalisation at Scarborough which included the absorption of the Hardwick business into that of Scarborough & District, the former's depot at Snainton was closed on 26 March and at the same time, the old Wallace Arnold garage at Columbus Ravine, Scarborough was vacated leaving the Hardwicks fleet based at the town's Westwood coach park.

Having enjoyed a period of comparative calm since deregulation in October 1986, East Yorkshire suddenly found themselves facing competition from several new or expanding independents in the Hull and Bridlington areas, and after regaining their monopoly of Scarborough's sea front following their acquisition of Hardwick's, suddenly found they had a new predator when P.K. Historic Omnibus Co. who were based at Hunmanby, began operations along the sea front using a selection of historic open-top double deckers. In the event however, P.K's threat was short lived and after falling foul of the Traffic Commissioner following the unsatisfactory operation of their services, their operators licence was revoked and they ceased trading on 28 July prior to going into voluntary liquidation.

One of the most unexpected and surprising developments of 1988 was the purchase of 8 former London Buses Routemasters in April, 7 of which were acquired for operation, the other for spares. Five of these were painted into East Yorkshire's traditional indigo blue & primrose livery by Kent Engineering before their delivery to Hull and one was similarly treated by London Buses Edgware garage, the remaining vehicle being painted by its new owner at the Anlaby Common workshops. Obtained for use on the busy and long established 56/56A routes in Hull from Ferensway coach station to Bilton/Longhill in competition with David Coster's Citilink and Kingston upon Hull City Transport, the Routemasters took up their duties on 2 May and immediately proved popular with passengers and staff alike.

The Routemasters were not the only unusual vehicles to be added to the fleet however, for in June a Duple-bodied 29-seat Bedford OB coach was acquired from Tours, Isle of Man. Bought for semi preservation and for private hire work on special occasions, this was repainted into the old primrose and riviera blue livery and was re--registered KSU381, its Manx number having to be forfeited. Also joining the fleet at this same time was an Alexander-bodied Leyland Atlantean acquired from London Country North East (yet another member of the AJS Group) but which had begun life with Strathclyde PTE.

The Bristol RELL mobile office which during the winter had been used as a waiting room at Ferensway coach station, Hull was released to return to its more customary duties at the beginning of May, its role at Ferensway passing to a withdrawn Leyland National. Departures from the fleet saw

*Over the years, a variety of East Yorkshire's withdrawn vehicles have ended their days in use as a left luggage room at Ferensway Coach Station, Hull. In January 1989 this duty was being undertaken by a time-expired Leyland National. (K.A.Jenkinson)*

one of the dual purpose Iveco 49.10 minis leave in April for a period of hire to West Yorkshire Road Car Co. and upon its return in June, it was immediately sold to London Country North East. Another vehicle to join West Yorkshire in May, albeit on this occasion permanently, was one of Scarborough & District's open-top Bristol VRTs which was required by its new owner for use on a tourist service in Bronteland.

*One of Northern general's Park Royal-bodied Atlanteans which were converted to open-top configuration for an aborted order from a customer in the middle-east, OTY403M was acquired by East Yorkshire in 1988. Placed in service in the Scarborough & District fleet, it is seen here wearing an all-cream livery for use on the sea-front service in this coastal resort. (P.J.S.Shipp)*

Scarborough & District's former United Plaxton-bodied Leyland Leopard 23 enjoys the summer sunshine in July 1988 as it rests in Whitby bus station while undertaking a private hire duty. (K.A.Jenkinson)

Travelling along Ferensway, Hull enroute to the city's eastern suburbs on service 56A on 12 May 1988, former London Routemaster 804 (WLT982) had only been in service in its new home for a few days and had not yet received the white band around the edges of its roof. (R.J.Waterhouse)

Scarborough & District 401 (CYC461A, originally LHE126W) was a Reeve Burgess-bodied Mercedes Benz L508D 19-seat coach acquired with the Wallace Arnold Scarborough operations in 1987. Seen here outside the EYMS Group's central workshops at Anlaby Common, it wore a predominantly white livery. (P.J.S.Shipp)

Transferred to the Hardwicks fleet in 1988 is former Scarborough & District Robin Hood-bodied Fiat 49.10 minicoach 37, seen in its 'new owner's' livery at Ferensway bus park, Hull on 7 April 1989. (K.A.Jenkinson)

One of the Scarborough & District Reeve Burgess-bodied Mercedes L609D acquired with United's operations in 1986, 414 is seen here after being repainted into its new owner's silver, red & blue 'Scarborough Skipper' livery. (T.Carter)

# MORE INDEPENDENTS SUCCUMB

Further expansion was achieved on 3 June when East Yorkshire purchased the vehicles and contracts of Phillips Coach Co. of Shiptonthorpe near Market Weighton. This added 14 more vehicles to the company's fleet and gave them fourteen schools contracts covering a large area of North Humberside. Phillips' Shiptonthorpe premises were not included in the deal.

Clive Harry Chorley Phillips had entered the field of bus and coach operation in September 1952 when he purchased a pair of secondhand Bedford buses - an OWB and an OB - and undertook schools contract work. Doubling the size of his fleet during the following year with the acquisition of another secondhand Bedford OWB and a 1938 Bedford WTB, his fleet gradually grew to more than 50 vehicles which were employed on a wide range of contract duties. One of the most memorable features of Phillips' fleet was that it comprised wholly of secondhand elderly vehicles of a wide range of makes and models and the fact that no new vehicles were ever purchased. Similarly, after their withdrawal, vehicles were rarely sold and were instead left to decompose in the large field behind his depot at Shiptonthorpe. Despite having large premises, a large number of Phillips' vehicles were each night parked at the side of roads around North Humberside near the homes of their drivers rather than being stabled at Shiptonthorpe !

The operational vehicles taken over from Phillips by East Yorkshire comprised 3 Leyland Tiger Cubs; 6 Bristol RELLs; 1 Bristol LH6L and one each Bedford VAS; SB5; YRQ and J2Z. All retained their former operator's red & cream livery and continued in operation on their customary contract duties.

More strangers arrived when East Yorkshire on 13 June received on loan from Premier Travel, Cambridge, a Duple-bodied Leyland Tiger coach. This remained in North Humberside until 28 July when it returned home. The need for additional coach-seated high capacity double deckers for use on the company's longer distance services led to the purchase in August of 4 ECW-bodied long wheelbase Leyland Olympian 69-seaters from London Country North East. Arriving in Green Line's Flightline livery, these were given their new owner's corporate white and two-tone blue colours before their entry into service and at first they were mainly used on the 121 service from Hull to Scarborough.

*One of several former Burnley & Pendle East Lancs-bodied Leyland Tiger Cubs operated by Phillips, Shiptonthorpe, BHG361C did not survive long enough to pass to East Yorkshire with the Phillips business in 1988.*
*(T. W. W. Knowles)*

*Above : Acquired in 1986 with United's operations, Scarborough & District's depot in Vernon Road, Scarborough was built on two levels, the lower of which was confined to single deck vehicles. In more recent times, this property has been sold and the company's fleet in now housed at a new site on the fringe of the town.*
*(T. Carter)*

*One of four ECW coach-bodied Leyland Olympians acquired from London Country North East in 1988, 545 (B109LPH) approaches York railway station on a journey to Hull on the 746 service in April 1989.*
*(K.A. Jenkinson)*

*Freshly repainted in Scarborough & District livery, ex.United ECW-bodied Leyland Olympian 541 passes Bridlington depot enroute to Scarborough on the 122 service on 18 July 1988. (K.A.Jenkinson)*

*Leyland National 101 (1918KH, originally NPD124L), acquired from London Country North East in 1988, was converted for the carriage of disabled passengers by the addition of wheelchair access in the centre of its nearside. Painted in a predominantly white livery, it is seen here at Ferensway bus park, Hull in 1989,    (K.A.Jenkinson)*

*One of a pair of MCW Metroliner double deck coaches purchased in 1986, 18 is pictured here after being repainted from its original National Express-style colours of white with red & blue bands into its owner's standard coach livery of white and two-tone blue.    (P.J.S.Shipp)*

*Leaving the Asda terminus of route 56 at Longhill in February 1989, former London Routemaster 807 (366CLT) with its white edged roof became the first of its type to loose its registration number in favour of a new 'A' suffixed identity. (K.A.Jenkinson)*

Joining these from the same source was a Leyland National which had been converted for the carriage of the disabled and was fitted with a wheelchair ramp in the nearside of its body. Leaving the fleet at this time were a pair of Leyland National 2s which were sold to East Midland Motor Services Ltd. and another Iveco minibus which departed south to join some of its sisters in the fleet of London Country North East.

On 16 September, a Plaxton-bodied Leyland Tiger coach was hired from Premier Travel, staying until 2 November whilst a Scarborough & District ECW-bodied Olympian and a Leyland National 2 were both transferred to East Yorkshire at Hull, the latter retaining its Hardwicks livery which was then given East Yorkshire fleet names. Also in September, a helping hand was offered to West Yorkshire Road Car Co. Ltd. who found themselves desperately short of double deck buses with which to operate schools contracts in the Leeds and Keighley areas. To help alleviate this situation, East Yorkshire loaned them 6 Bristol VRTs which spent several weeks in West Yorkshire before returning home to Hull.

A new minibus service was inaugurated on 16 November, albeit on an experimental basis, running from Beverlay to Hull and serving Hull Pier and the city's marina. Marketed under the title of 'Hull Mariner', this proved quite popular and was well patronised from the start. Having a shortage of minibuses at that time, East Yorkshire hired a Carlyle-bodied Ford Transit from West Yorkshire Road Car Co. Ltd. for use on this new operation, the vehicle in question retaining its rightful owner's blue 'Hoppa' livery.

The bad news in 1988 was a two-week strike by Hull-based drivers and conductors. This dispute arose during the annual wage negotiations and was the first significant industrial action at East Yorkshire since 1966, disturbing the good industrial relations which have been notable at the company both before and since, although a one-week strike in the spring of the following year at Scarborough was another unfortunate 'hiccup'.

Although 1989 began quietly, it was to prove to be a most eventful year with the company experiencing new competition in several areas, numerous fleet changes and further expansion and consolidation.

During January, the Ford Transit minibus hired in November from West Yorkshire was purchased together with

At one time the only double decker in the Cherry's fleet, former Northern General Park Royal-bodied Leyland Atlantean 609 (OTY409M) gained its all-over cream livery upon its transfer from East Yorkshire in 1988. (K.A.Jenkinson)

In 1989 East Yorkshire purchased two Carlyle-bodied Ford Transit minibuses from West Yorkshire Road Car Co.Ltd. One of these, 321 (D535HNW) still in its former owner's blue. orange & cream 'Hoppa' livery but with 'Little Bus' fleet names, waits in Hull prior to departing for Beverley. (EYMS)

An unusual vehicle in the East Yorkshire fleet is open-top ECW-bodied Bristol RELL 600 which was converted to this form by United from whom it was acquired with that company's Scarborough operations in 1986. It is seen here in its current owner's indigo blue & primrose livery carrying the name 'Sea Princess'. (P.J.S.Shipp)

a second vehicle of this type from the same source whilst the now customary transfer of vehicles between the Group's subsidiaries continued. Four months later, 2 of East Yorkshire's Leyland Tiger coaches together with 1 from Scarborough & District were sold to the newly-formed National Express subsidiary, Dorset Travel Services of Bournemouth while 3 of Scarborough & District's Leyland Nationals and one of their dual purpose Leopards were loaned to West Yorkshire Road Car Co. in March/April to assist that company over a period of vehicle shortages.

Following their expansion plans, the EYMS Group acquired the business and vehicles of Cottingham Mini Coaches on 29 April, adding some specialist operations to their fold and increasing their fleet by 8 vehicles. These comprised a 35-seat Ford R1014; 2 Mercedes L307D 12-seaters; 1 MAN 27-seat coach; 1 14-seat Fiat 35.8; 1 Dormobile bodied 19-seat Talbot and a pair of non-PSV Volkswagen minibuses, all of which wore Cottingham's off-white, yellow, orange & brown livery.

Cottingham Mini Coaches was formed in April 1976 by Maurice Lawton of 1 Newgate Street, Cottingham. Starting with a 12-seat Deansgate-bodied Ford Transit, Lawton offered a service from his home area to Manchester Airport on a door-to-door basis and as this operation gained in popularity, additional vehicles were purchased. Eventually, the airport service was expanded to operate every four hours, day and night and in addition, a private hire business was also built up which resulted in the purchase of a larger capacity coach.

Although the EYMS Group formed a new company - Cottingham Mini Coaches Ltd. - to acquire Lawton's business, this was based at Cherry's Springfield Way premises at Anlaby from which the vehicles were operated. In June, the Cottingham company was fully absorbed by

One of the vehicles taken over with the business of Cottingham Mini Coaches (but not retained for long by its new owner) was UAG88W, a non-PSV Volkswagen which was mainly used on duties to and from Manchester Airport. (P.J.S.Shipp)

Purchased new for the Cottingham Mini Coaches fleet in 1990 was G214RKH, a 19-seat Whittaker-bodied Mercedes Benz 811D which is seen here before its entry into service. (EYMS)

One of the vehicles ultimately acquired with the operations of Yesteryear Travel was FHW156D, an ECW-bodied Bristol MW6G coach which began life with Bristol Omnibus Co. in 1966.    (EYMS)

Cherry Coaches after operating on East Yorkshire discs since April, although the Cottingham Mini Coaches trading name was retained and carried by the vehicles which were still maintained in their distinctive yellow & white livery. By this time, Pheonix Radio Taxis Ltd. had lost their only PSV (which had recently been transferred to Cottingham Mini Coaches) and now concentrating solely on the operation of taxicabs, it came as no great surprise when, in June, the company was sold to its manager, Paul Cassidy. Phillips Coaches operators licence was also surrendered in June at which time this fleet was also integrated into the Cherry Coaches operation.

Meanwhile, Scarborough & District's activities were far from healthy in both their home town and Bridlington where mounting competition from other operators was creaming off a significant amount of business. This caused the company to close its depot in St.John Street, Bridlington and to lease some Health Authority premises behind the houses on the opposite side of the same street as a replacement. The new 'depot' was only suitable for minibuses however and the move was therefore only possible following the withdrawal of the last of the 'big buses' from Bridlington, although a couple have since returned and are parked elsewhere in the town. Following its closure, the company's original depot was sold to Kwik-Fit Motorists Centres. In Scarborough, the sea-front service was once again the focal point for competition with Applebys and Primrose Valley, both of whom offered a strong challenge to Scarborough & District's established open-top service. In addition Primrose Valley also registered services to Cayton Village and Eastfield and one to Bridlington, all of which ran in direct competition to the established company, as did a service provided by a comparatively new operator, Four Oaks Travel. In an attempt to stem the tide, Scarborough & District entered into an agreement with Yesteryear Travel, a company set up by Silver Service of Darley Dale, Derbyshire, to operate period vehicles on Scarborough's sea-front service and also on private hire duties. Yesteryear Travel had been formed following the collapse of P.K. Historic Omnibus Co. and used an open top former Lancaster Leyland PD2, an open-top ex.Lincolnshire Road Car Co. Bristol FS6G Lodekka and an ECW coach-bodied Bristol MW6G which had begun life with Bristol Omnibus Co. All three vehicles wore an attractive silver & blue livery and had previously served in the erstwhile P.K. fleet. Taking up their new duties on 1 June, they continued to operate until 3 September. In addition to all these developments, Scarborough & District undertook a massive revision of its operations in its home town under which all its conventional-size buses with the exception of its open-top double deckers were replaced by 23 new Reeve Burgess-bodied Mercedes 709D and 811D midibuses leased from Roadlease Ltd. These joined the 14 Mercedes minibuses inherited from United in 1986 and were housed at the comany's depots in Beaconsfield Street and Vernon Road, despite the latter being under the threat of closure.

The Bristol VRTs, Olympians and Leyland Nationals replaced in Scarborough were all cascaded to East Yorkshire Motor Services for continued operation (at first retaining Scarborough & District's red & grey livery, albeit with East Yorkshire fleet names), their arrival in North Humberside allowing a number of the company's secondhand double deckers to be withdrawn for disposal. The remaining three new Mercedes midibuses leased from Roadlease were placed in the East Yorkshire fleet and were allocated to Beverley to replace the Ford Transits on the town services there.

Following the temporary departure of a Plaxton Paramount-bodied Leyland Tiger coach which was hired by East Yorkshire to Rover Coaches of Worcester for two weeks in June, a further five former London Routemasters were added to the fleet. Of these, 2 were purchased in July from Kingston upon Hull City Transport for whom they had never operated since their acquisition from Citilink, Hull in March 1989, the remaining three coming from Lincolnshire Road Car Co. Ltd. in July and previously having been operated by Gash of Newark.

Routemaster 810 (WLT757) acquired from Road Car, Lincoln in 1989 was at first operated by Scarborough & District still wearing its former Gash, Newark two-tone green & cream livery. It is seen here in Scarborough whilst operating the Cloughton service.   (G.T.W.Carter)

*Seen when new in 1989, Reeve Burgess-bodied Mercedes Benz 709D 443 poses with its two sisters before entering service in Beverley in 'Little Bus' silver, blue & red livery. (P.J.S.Shipp)*

*Originally registered XPM42 and owned by Brighton Hove & District, 1962 open-top Bristol FS6G AFE170A was acquired by Scarborough & District in 1989 with the operations of Yesteryear Travel in whose livery it is seen here at Corner Cafe, Scarborough while operating the sea-front service in 1990. (T.Carter)*

West Yorkshire Group in September, one going to Keighley & District, the other to York City & District for driver training purposes. In the event, both saw occasional use in normal service however and although 307 returned home from Keighley in October, its sister - 305 - remained at York until the end of the year when it was then sold to York City & District who placed it in normal revenue-earning service.

Following experiments with ex.Scarborough & District Bristol VRTs 721 and 725 in October, East Yorkshire adopted the former's red & portland grey as their standard bus livery in place of the previous red & white colours, although the coaches were to retain their attractive white and two-tone blue styling and the Routemasters were to keep the company's old colours of indigo blue & primrose. At around this same time, the former United Mercedes minibuses of Scarborough & District lost their old Scarborough Skipper livery in favour of East Yorkshire's standard minibus hue of silver, blue & red whilst coach-seated Olympian 532 upon its down-grading to normal bus duties lost its white & blue colours in favour of the new standard red & portland grey. Ancillary vehicle 848, a Leyland Panther former bus which had latterly served as a mobile publicity vehicle, was loaned under a two-year agreement to Yorkshire Regional Newspapers as a promotional vehicle advertising various Scarborough district newspapers, although it remained available for use by East Yorkshire as required whilst the Bristol RELL mobile travel office had been given

July 1989 brought the announcement of the decision to finally close East Yorkshire's central repair workshops at Anlaby Common and to transfer all heavy maintenance work etc. to the company's Anlaby Road depot at Hull where additional land had recently been acquired. The Anlaby Common premises were then sold and have since been demolished to make way for a sheltered housing scheme. Also witnessed was the departure of Alan Stephenson from the EYMS Group Ltd. to allow him to concentrate his energies on his AJS Group of companies. After relinquishing his shareholding in the company, his position as Chairman was taken by Peter Shipp who also became Managing Director (Operations) whilst the other original buy-out director Godfrey Burley, who was also the Company Secretary, became Managing Director (Finance).

Returning to the fleet, in order to maintain new schools contracts which required double deckers, three of the recently-acquired Routemasters were transferred to Scarborough & District early in September. One retained its former Citilink blue & silver livery and one its Gash colour scheme of two-tone green & cream whilst the third was repainted in Scarborough & District's red & white and in addition to being employed on schools duties, all three were frequently used on Scarborough's town services where, being conductor operated, they immediately became favourites amongst passengers. At this same time, one of East Yorkshire's ex.Scarborough & District Bristol VRTs was transferred to the Cherry fleet at for a variety of duties and was the first bus of this type to be permanently allocated to this subsidiary. Prior to these happenings, Scarborough & District had purchased the three vehicles operated in the town in conjunction with Yesteryear Travel. On a less happy note, coach-seated ECW-bodied Olympian 533 met with disaster when on 13 August it collided with the steel canopy outside Bridlington District Hospital, causing severe damage to its front upper deck and roof. The vehicle normally used on this contract was one of the company's minibuses .... need more be said !

Having by now a small surplus of older-type minibuses, a pair of Carlyle-converted Ford Transits were loaned to the

*Although currently on loan to Yorkshire Regional Newspapers for promotional purposes, Marshall-bodied Leyland Panther 848 (MAT848F) is still owned by Scarborough & District. (EYMS)*

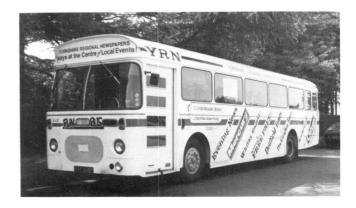

*Representing East Yorkshire's preserved fleet is Bedford OB KSU381, Leyland LT2 DV7890 and AEC Regent V VKH44 with Roe Beverley Bar-roofed body. (P.J.S.Shipp)*

Scarborough & District names and was used during the summer at Valley Bridge bus station, Scarborough and later as the Skipper office at Bridlington.

During the summer of 1989, an experimental service had been inaugurated under the title 'Flamborough Headlander' running from Sewerby to the Headland area and using two Hornsea-based Ford Transit minibuses. Subsidised by Humberside County Council, East Yorkshire Borough Council and the Countryside Commission, such was the success of this seasonal service that it was operated again in 1990. Later in the year, after the summer operations had ended in Scarborough, Appleby's launched three new commercially operated town services in order to retain their staff and presence in the town. Using 5 coaches, these attacked some of Scarborough & District's most lucrative routes and adding to their mounting difficulties, Primrose Valley began a half-hourly service between Scarborough & Claughton in November and Four Oaks Travel began hourly operations to Cayton. To counter Primrose Valley's new operation, Scarborough & District placed two of their Routemasters on their own Claughton service in an attempt to stop the defection of passengers.

More departures and arrivals were witnessed before the year ended when a pair of Leyland National 2s were sold during November to Caldaire Holdings of Wakefield for use in their Yorkshire Woollen District Transport fleet. In the opposite direction, Cherry Coaches acquired in December an ECW bus-bodied Bristol LH6L single decker from Northern General Transport who had used it as a driver training

vehicle, but more interestingly East Yorkshire added yet another vintage vehicle to their special duties fleet. This was a 1931 Leyland LT2 fitted with a 1947 Burlingham coach body which was acquired from Kirkby Central (dealers) of Anston who had restored it several years earlier. Placed in use in the spring of 1990, it kept in its acquired cream & blue livery, this being judged sufficiently similar to East Yorkshire's traditional coach livery to not justify its

*An odd man out in the East Yorkshire fleet is Alexander-bodied Leyland Atlantean 876 (KSU876P). Seen here at Ferensway bus park, Hull, it was acquired from London Country North East in 1988 but began life with Strathclyde PTE. (EYMS)*

*Much-travelled Routemaster 809 (741DYE) is seen here freshly repainted in Scarborough & District livery working a duty on the local service to Cloughton in the spring of 1991. (EYMS)*

*East Yorkshire extensively refurbished 952, one of its 1974 Park Royal-bodied Leyland Atlanteans, to extend its life for a further six years. Fitted with a new-style front and electronic destination equipment, it was intended that further buses would be similarly treated, but the scheme was abandoned in view of the high costs involved. (EYMS)*

*Awaiting its passengers in Hull while working competitive service 121 is Revill of Driffield's former Northern General Leyland National GPT97N which, following the collapse of that company was purchased by East Yorkshire for spares. (K.A.Jenkinson)*

*Hurrying through Woodmansey on its way from Beverley to Hull on the 121 service is 812 (ALM65B), an ex.London Routemaster which had served with Gash, Newark before passing to Lincolnshire Road Car Co. from whom it was acquired in 1989. (K.A.Jenkinson)*

*TUP5E, a Plaxton-bodied Bedford VAS1 of 1967 vintage was acquired with the business of Phillips, Shiptonthorpe in 1989 and was then placed in the Cherry Coaches fleet where it is seen here still wearing its previous owner's red & cream livery. (EYMS)*

immediate repainting. Finally, in an attempt to extend the life of a number of its older Atlantean double deckers, East Yorkshire despatched Park Royal-bodied 952 to Kirkby Central at Anston for refurbishing in December. This included the fitting of a new, restyled front panel; electronic destination equipment; new floors and some new pillars and at a cost of around £15,000 it was believed that this would give the bus a further six years life. Although it had originally been intended to extend this treatment to several other double decker in the fleet, it was felt that the higher cost of similar refurbishments could not be justified and as a result no further vehicles were treated in this manner.

In order to counter an assault made upon the Hull to Beverley section of East Yorkshire's 121 Hull to Scarborough service by Revills of Langtoft near Driffield, East Yorkshire introduced Routemasters onto the part of this service under attack, this being a move which quickly proved popular with passengers who prefered this type of vehicle to the varied selection of buses and coaches offered by Revills. In February 1990, the threat from this predator suddenly disappeared when Driffield & District (Revills) called in the receivers and ceased trading. The sudden demise of this operator whose 16 vehicles had been employed on school contracts, stage carriage services and private hire duties left North Yorkshire County Council and Humberside County Council to urgently seek another operator to maintain their schools contracts and these were quickly rewarded to East Yorkshire on a temporary basis until August 1990. Although not particularly short of vehicles, the EYMS Group acquired three of Revills' vehicles from the Receiver in March, a Plaxton-bodied Bedford VAS coach which they allocated to the Cherry fleet, an ex.West Midlands Daimler Fleetline which went to Scarborough & District and a former Northern General Leyland National which East Yorkshire took to Hull for cannibalisation.

Undoubtedly, the first major event of the new decade was the purchase of Primrose Valley Coaches of Filey on 1 February 1990, thus eliminating some fierce competition in Scarborough and on the 121 service to Bridlington. In addition to consolidating the EYMS Group's position this brought a further 18 vehicles into their fold, these being 3 Beford YRTs; 1 each Bedford YMT and YNT; 4 Ford R1114s; 1 Leyland Leopard and 8 Leyland/Daimler Fleetlines originating from London Buses and West Midlands Travel.

Started by Alfred James and Annie Horsley Coates and Archibald William and Esme Elley in June 1951, Primrose Valley Coaches began their operations with a solitary Duple-bodied Bedford OB coach, using this on a seasonal Saturdays only service from Filey to Primrose Valley caravan park and using it on other days on excursions from Filey. The company's close proximity to Butlin's Holiday Camp brought them additional business and in 1953/4 the fleet grew from one to five coaches, all of which were purchased second hand and were of a variety of makes and types, their only common factor being their red & cream livery. Further excursions were begun from Reighton during the 'sixties as

were a daily summer service from Filey bus station to Primrose Valley camp via Reighton Gap and an express service from Filey to the Gaiety Theatre, Scarborough and by 1970 the fleet had grown to 7 coaches. In 1973, the Coates family sold their share of the business to Albert Webster and in addition to the coaching operation, a petrol station and car repair business was also maintained from the company's premises in Primrose valley Road, Filey. Webster purchased Elley's holding in 1982 and was then joined by more members of his family who together built up the bus and coach operation and ventured into further local bus services upon deregulation in October 1986.

The deal agreed with Primrose Valley Coaches included the operations, vehicles and Filey premises of that company but did not involve the petrol station, car repair and electrical parts of the business which remained in the hands of the Webster family. Although the EYMS Group formed a new company under the title of Primrose Valley Coaches Ltd. and intended to maintain this as a separate subsidiary, until their new operators licence was granted, the acquired vehicles were operated on Scarborough & District discs.

Following closely on the heels of this new acquisition, Appleby's increased their competition in the Scarborough area by gaining the tendered North Yorkshire County Council service 119 from Scarborough to Hunmanby which had previously been in the hands of Scarborough & District. Applebys also announced that it was their intention to operate 6 open-top double deckers on a 10-minute frequency along Scarborough's sea front for the duration of the summer season and in addition, to use 9 coaches on excursion and private hire duties in the Scarborough area in 1990 as well as continue to maintain their existing town services to Eastfield, Briercliffe and Scalby. To this end a lease was taken on premises at Four Oaks farm outside Scarborough from which all these vehicles would operate.

Although the EYMS Group fleet was comparatively stable at the start of 1990, in February a secondhand ECW-bodied Bristol LH6L was acquired from Tyne & Wear Omnibus Co. for use in the Cherry fleet and during this same month East Yorkshire repurchased one of their former buses which had been sold for preservation in April 1972. This was a Willowbrook-bodied AEC Regent V with 'Beverley Bar' roof which had first entered service with the company in 1956. Already restored in its original livery, it was added to East Yorkshire's 'special events' fleet after receiving attention to return it to PSV standards it was licensed for use in June.

Following the acquisition of Primrose Valley Coaches, the EYMS Group further consolidated its position in Scarborough by purchasing another of its competitors, Four Oaks Travel of Seamer who operated a service between Scarborough and Cayton and one from Warner's Holiday Village at Cayton Bay. Four Oaks' 2 coaches, a Leyland Leopard and a Bedford YMT, both of which carried Plaxton bodywork, were acquired with the business and were then added to the Primrose Valley fleet although on this occasion no premises were involved in the deal, those used by Four Oaks having

been on lease. Before very long, both the newly-acquired services were integrated into those already operated by Scarborough & District.

A comparatively new company, Four Oaks Travel was started in December 1988 by Terence William Campling, John Robert Porter and Michael Lawrence Scholefield. Operating from leased premises at Four Oaks Farm on Seamer Road, the business never grew beyond two vehicles, the first of which was the Bedford still owned at the time of the take over by the EYMS Group, and another being a former Greater Manchester Leyland Atlantean which had been acquired from Black Prince, Morley whose colours it retained during its period with Four Oaks.

April saw Scarborough & District in the news yet again when, after several weeks of speculation, the town centre two storey depot in Vernon Road which had been inherited from United in 1986 was closed and its allocation moved to a new site at Dunslow Road, Eastfield on the fringe of the town. The former Wallace Arnold garage at Beaconsfield Street, Scarborough was also closed, leaving all Scarborough & District's vehicles housed at the new depot, although the company still occupied the Westwood bus park next to Scarborough Railway Station, whose lease from British Rail had been inherited from United

*Seen in the red & primrose livery in which it was acquired with the business of Four Oaks Travel, Scarborough in 1990 is Plaxton-bodied Leyland Leopard AJO311R. Although placed in its new owner's Primrose Valley Coaches fleet, for a short time it still carried details painted on its bodywork of the erstwhile Four Oaks stage carriage service.   (EYMS)*

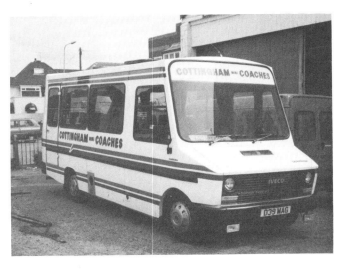

*Originally operated by East Yorkshire, Robin Hood coach-bodied Fiat 49.10 39 (D39MAG) was transferred to the Cottingham Mini Coaches fleet in 1989 and repainted into their livery.   (P.J.S.Shipp)*

The need by East Yorkshire for additional double deckers pending the delivery of 6 new NCME-bodied Leyland Olympians during the late summer led the company to once again turn to the secondhand market and in April, a PDR1A/1R-type Leyland Atlantean was purchased from Cleveland Transit. Although the chassis of this bus dated from 1970, it had been refurbished by its owners and brought up to AN68 specification, whilst its NCME body was only six years old and as a result, looked extremely modern. After repainting it into their red & portland grey fleet livery, East Yorkshire placed it in service towards the end of May, by which time a further two buses of this same type had been purchased from Cleveland Transit with two more following early in June. Only one of these gained its new operator's livery before being placed in service however, the remaining three retaining their former owner's green, yellow & white colours - albeit with East Yorkshire fleet names - for several weeks until repainting could take place. In order to disguise their age, all five buses were re-registered with Irish numbers during August and September. At around this same time, a decision was taken to offer some of the company's Routemaster registration numbers for sale and to this end, several were advertised through a dealer in this field although they were at that time all still carried by the buses concerned. Although they did not attract buyers with the speed that was at first anticipated, the registration of 807 (366CLT) quickly found an interested party when it was purchased as a birthday present for Claire Louise Trott for use on her car. As a result, 807 was re-registered NKH807A. The only new vehicle to arrive during April 1990 was a Mercedes Benz MB811D Eurpoa-bodied 19-seat coach which was allocated to the Cottingham Mini Coaches fleet.

*Freshly repainted into its new owner's colours, former Cleveland Transit NCME-rebodied Leyland Atlantean 917 is seen here outside Hull railway station soon after its entry into service in 1990. Still carrying its original identity SDC138H, it was soon afterwards reregistered NJI1250 to disguise the true age of its chassis.   (K.A.Jenkinson)*

*Still wearing the green, white & yellow colours of its former owner, Cleveland Transit but fitted with East Yorkshire fleet names is NCME-rebodied Leyland Atlantean 920 (SDC144H) which after running in this form for a few weeks was repainted into standard red & portland grey livery and reregistered NJI1253.   (P.J.S.Shipp)*

A new operation gained by East Yorkshire in May was a service sponsored by Humberside County Council and Hull City Council which linked Hull's Victoria Pier with the city's markets and the coach station at Ferensway. Numbered 50, this was operated on a 20 minute frequency by three of the company's preserved vehicles - the Bedford OB, Leyland LT2 and the 'Beverley Bar' AEC Regent V. East Yorkshire's operation on this new service was however confined to Sundays, the Monday to Saturday journeys being provided by Kingston upon Hull City Transport.

Further consolidation was achieved when, in May, the EYMS Group took over the service run by Hull travel agent, Travelplan, which ran 'on demand' from the city to Manchester International Airport together with Travelplan's two Freight Rover Sherpa minicoaches. Placed under the control of EYMS subsidiary, Cottingham Mini Coaches, this service was integrated into Cottingham's established regular summer service to the airport and at the same time, an experimental service was inaugurated between Hull and East Midlands Airport.

An unexpected bonus was gained by East Yorkshire during June when, as a result of a crippling three week strike by the staff of Kingston upon Hull City Transport, the company was awarded 10 Humberside County Council school contracts on an emergency basis which between them required 15 buses. This somewhat stretched East Yorkshire's resources and as a temporary measure, three ECW-bodied Bristol VRTs were hired from Yorkshire Traction in addition to the ex.Cleveland Atlanteans being pressed into service before repainting as mentioned earlier. Despite the municipal buses being 'off the

road' from 7 June, East Yorkshire and other local independents were unable to step in to provide replacement services as a result of the Traffic Commissioner refusing to waive the 42-day rule applied to service licensing. Almost as soon as the City Transport strike ended, two of the Yorkshire Traction buses departed to rejoin their rightful owner, the third being retained for a few more days until its eventual return early in July.

Finding their new activities in Scarborough had not come up to their expectations, Applebys rationalised their operations in that area in June and on the final day of that month withdrew all their services except that to Scalby and the open-top operation along the sea-front. Similarly, they pruned their coaching activities in the town, but registered two new local services to start on 16 July which were designed to cover more efficiently some of the areas they had previously served. Resulting from these moves, Applebys' Scarborough-based fleet was reduced to 5 open-top double deckers, 1 excursion cosch and 2 single deck buses. Although this weakened their competition towards Scarborough & District, the latter were still suffering losses and in an attempt to stem these, in June transferred almost all of their coaching operations to their associated Primrose Valley company. This left Scarborough & District retaining only its National Express contracted workings on the 320 service to Swansea (which was jointly operated with National Welsh) and its two National Express-liveried coaches. Later, on 19 August, a further rationalisation of Scarborough & District's local bus services resulted in a tightening-up of

schedules and reduction of frequencies to produce a reduced vehicle requirement. One silver lining to the dark clouds however was the gaining of a tender from Scarborough Borough Council for the operation of a free weekend park and ride service from Weaponness Coach Park to Aquarium Top, this being operated with Skipper minibuses on a 10-minute frequency between 10.00am and 6.00pm from July to September. Partly as a result of these changes, Scarborough & District withdrew its three Routemasters from service, transferring two to East Yorkshire and placing the third in store. One of the pair moving to Hull was however quickly hired to South Yorkshire Transport (from 27 June) for use on a high-frequency and busy route in Doncaster which was more usually operated by minibuses and which was at that time being contested by Wilfreda-Beehive of Adwick. Wearing its rightful owner's immaculate red & white livery and fleet names with the addition of 'SYT' logos to its front upper deck bulkhead windows, 810 (WLT757) quickly proved successful in its new adopted home and offering passengers a touch of nostalgia - and crew operation - attracted good loadings on almost every journey.

During July, East Yorkshire modified one of their ECW-bodied Bristol VRTs (519) by fitting it with several DPTAC features such as a low entrance step and extra handrails etc. to meet the needs of less able-bodied passengers. Adapted to meet the special requirements of Humberside County Council for contracts won by the company which were to start in September, four more VRTs were similarly modified during August whilst the six new Olympians were also equipped to DPTAC specification. The services upon which the VRTs were to be used were from Walkington to Beverley; Thwing to Bridlington; .Driffield to Langtoft and Beverley to Hornsea, although they were to be also to be used on a number of the company's other services too. July also witnessed the transfer of a former West Midlands Daimler Fleetline from the Scarborough & District fleet to Primrose Valley where it replaced a former London Transport Fleetline whilst East Yorkshire evaluated a Leyland Lynx for a couple of weeks in July, this being obtained from VL Bus & Coach who in turn had hired it from Welsh municipal operator, Cynon Valley. This was followed by a DAF-Optare 'Delta' demonstrator, the main purpose of the trials being to see if either bus would be suitable as a replacement for the Leopard coaches used on Scarborough & District's single deck routes between Scarborough, Pickering and Helmsley.

August witnessed the entry into service of the first brand-new double deckers to join the EYMS Group since its privatisation, these being six long wheelbase Leyland Olympians with Cummins engines and NCME 85-seat bodies. Painted in East Yorkshire's standard red & portland grey livery, to which had, since May 1990, been added matt black 'skirt' panels, they were allocated to Hull depot for use on the busy services from the city to Hessle. In addition, East Yorkshire also received a trio of new Volvo coaches with Plaxton Expressliner 46-seat coachwork into which was incorporated a servery and toilet. Painted in National Express Rapide livery, these three coaches were obtained for operation on the contracted service between Hull and London. A further vehicle arriving in August was a Dormobile-bodied 29-seat Mercedes Benz 709D midibus which was borrowed for a couple of weeks from Derwent Vehicles of Leeds for evaluation.

Following their highly successful operation of Routemasters on their two services from Hull to Longhill and Bilton and on that from Hull to Beverley, East Yorkshire who were facing increased competition from Connor & Graham of Easington who had started a new hourly off-peak service from Hull to Withernsea, retaliated on 10 September by providing extra journeys on their own 76 service from Hull as far as Thorngumbald, thus serving most of the main villages enroute, using a crew-operated Routemaster. Numbering this 'new' service 76Z, it operated along the main road from Hull to Thorngumbald and then entered the village, running on a one-way basis to rejoin the main road for its journey back to Hull. Four morning and one afternoon journeys were provided from Thorngumbald to the city with one morning

and four afternoon journeys being provided in the opposite direction. Operating every day except Sunday, the 76Z proved extremely popular amongst passengers and was well patronised. Meanwhile, several journeys on East Yorkshire's Driffield - Beeford - Hornsea and Driffield - Beeford - Bridlington services were deregistered due to the rapid decline in the number of passengers using them and as a result, a replacement network was devised by Humberside County Council which permitted through journeys using a series of contracted services. Although East Yorkshire managed to retain a few journeys under County Council contracts, most were gained by Ben Johnson of Brandesburton and Frodingham Coaches. Similarly, the contracted services in the Driffield area gained under emergency arrangements in April following the collapse of Revills were lost to Frodingham Coaches in September under the re-tendering process.

*Leyland Olympian 528 is pictured here in July 1990 after receiving an experimental livery which incorporated a narrow white band below its upper deck windows. (P.J.S.Shipp)*

These and other reductions in services enabled East Yorkshire to withdraw 5 of its Carlyle-bodied Ford Transit minibuses and Scarborough & District to likewise rid themselves of 3 buses of this type. Cherry Coaches withdrew a Leyland Leopard and a Ford R1114 while Primrose Valley placed in service the Plaxton-bodied 29-seat Bedford VAS coach acquired from Driffield & District and Scarborough & District upgraded two of its 20-seat bus-bodied Mercedes 608D minis by fitting them with 19 coach-type seats. The two then replaced the elderly Mercedes on the contract to provide coaches for the forces and civilian personnel who man the early-warning radar station on the North Yorkshire Moors. This contract, taken over with the Wallace Arnold acquisition in 1987, is unusual in that for security reasons the vehicles are always driven by site personnel rather than bus company drivers.

Further fleet changes were implemented during October when a further rebodied Atlantean was purchased by East Yorkshire from Cleveland Transit and 2 Bristol VRTs were acquired from Yorkshire Traction in exchange for a pair of Leyland Nationals. The Atlantean, like its predecessors was re-registered with a 'dateless' Irish number before its entry into service in November while of the Yorkshire Traction buses, one was placed in the East Yorkshire fleet in November whilst the other made its debut in December with Primrose Valley who also gained a Plaxton-bodied Leyland Leopard coach from the East Yorkshire fleet. Surplus to requirements by Scarborough & District, seven of the Reeve Burgess-bodied Mercedes minibuses inherited from United in 1986 were transferred to the East Yorkshire fleet for service in Bridlington where they ousted more of the original Ford Transits. Perhaps the most unexpected acquisition during October however was a former Western (Clydeside) Scottish Routemaster. Sadly this was not intended for operational use and was merely purchased as a source of spares for East Yorkshire's other buses of this type and after been stripped of all useful parts, it was subsequently sold for scrap.

*One of a pair of Reeve Burgess-bodied Iveco 49.10 minibuses purchased in 1990 for use on a new service in Goole, 447 pictured here, like its sister carried a special 'East Yorkshire Goole Town Bus' fleet name on its side panels. (P.J.S.Shipp)*

Two more Bristol VRTs arrived from Yorkshire Traction at the start of November and were joined by a further pair of rebodied Atlanteans from Cleveland Transit. One of the latter was given an Irish registration number before its entry into service in the East Yorkshire fleet whilst its sister retained its original identity, it being April of the following year before it too gained a dateless number. Both the 'Tracky' VRTs were allocated to the company's subsidiary fleets, one taking up its duties with Cherry Coaches in December in the all-white livery in which it had been received, the other being

repainted into East Yorkshire's red & portland grey colours before being despatched to join Primrose Valley. Four more of East Yorkshire's Routemasters were re-registered with A-suffix numbers which matched their fleet numbers, leaving only two of the original seven still sporting their London identities.

Hull independent operator Metro City Bus, who like the other main Hull independent Good News Travels (who trade as Humber Stagecoach on its bus routes), had continued to change services with regular frequency in order to 'cream-off' passengers from Kingston upon Hull City Transport on their most lucrative routes suddenly turned its attention towards East Yorkshire in December, starting an hourly service from Hull's city centre to Willerby. In response, the major company began a similar service between these two places numbered 44A, using on this a solitary Routemaster. The challenger, finding that their new service was perhaps not as profitable as had been initially believed, withdrew from the battle in March 1991, thus enabling East Yorkshire to discontinue its 44A service on 6 April, despite having received a petition from passengers who wished to retain their crew-operated service. Later in the year however the service returned, still Routemaster-operated, but with a slightly modified route. Although following the demise of Revills, East Yorkshire had continued to operate Routemasters on the 121 service between Hull and Beverley, these were withdrawn on 6 April when that service reverted to one-person-operation with journeys extended to Molescroft, a large estate on the north side of Beverley. Returning to 1990, East Yorkshire placed in service two new Reeve Burgess-bodied 25-seat Iveco 49.10 buses for use on a new Humberside County Council contract to provide a local town service in Goole. Painted in the company's standard mini/midibus livery of silver grey with a blue & red band and

*Delivered new in 1990 were a trio of Plaxton Expressliner-bodied Volvo B10M coaches which were painted in National Express Rapide livery for use on contracted services to that concern. Numbered 54, 55 & 56 they were registered H54VRH, H155VRH and H56VRH, the number H55VRH not being available to the company. (P.J.S.Shipp)*

*Purchased from Southend Transport in 1991 was 553, a two year-old Alexander-bodied Leyland Olympian which is seen here after being repainted into its new owner's colours but before modifications had been carried out to its destination box prior to being fitted with Bright-Tech electronic destination equipment. (EYMS)*

Seen in the all-cream livery in which it was received from Yorkshire Traction in 1990, Scarborough & District's ECW-bodied Bristol VRT 629 (HWE829N) is seen here at the Primrose Valley depot near Filey before being repainted into fleet livery. (P.J.S.Shipp)

carrying 'Goole Town Bus' fleet names, both buses were modified soon after purchase by lowering the entrance step to DiPTAC specification.

The new year opened with little or no change to the Group's operations or fleet, although it was not long before further expansionist plans were unveiled with the announcement that a new division had been formed within the Group to cater for the leisure market. This offered a new programme of rail-based excursions and holidays covering a wide range of destinations mainly in Great Britain but including a 5-day holiday to France. Designed to cater for travellers who preferred rail travel to journeys by coach or private car, the new division, named Rail UK, quickly attracted a healthy number of bookings thus justifying its creation. Further expansion took place in the early spring of 1991 when an additional vehicle was placed on the National Express contracted Hull - Liverpool service and a contract was gained from National Express for the provision of a vehicle on the Hull - Taunton service. In order to be able to undertake the latter, a fourth new Plaxton Expressliner-bodied Volvo B10M caoch was acquired on lease in February, painted in National Express Rapide livery. More surprising however was the arrival in this same month of a secondhand 'F; registered 75-seat Alexander-bodied Leyland Olympian which was purchased from Southend Transport and, after having its destination screen modified and receiving red & portland grey livery, was allocated to the East Yorkshire fleet.

Seeking additional double deckers and a means of updating some of the oldest parts of the fleet, attention was once again turned towards the secondhand market and resulted in a further two Yorkshire Traction ECW-bodied Bristol VRTs being acquired. One of these, retaining the all-white livery in which it arrived, was allocated to the Primrose Valley fleet while the other was despatched to Cherry Coaches where it replaced a former Yorkshire Traction bus of this same type which was then converted to open-top configuration for use by Scarborough & District on

the sea-front service in that resort. Cherry also withdrew its ex.Northern General Atlantean and the unique Caetano coach-bodied Fiat midicoach which had been acquired with Wallace Arnold's Scarborough operations and at this same time applied the appropriate lettering to its Plaxton-bodied Leopard 288 which was the regular vehicle used on the Leo's Supermarket free bus contract.

In Hull, East Yorkshire jointly sponsored a crime prevention campaign with Hull South Crime Prevention Panel in conjunction with Hull Police and Hull Safer Cities Project. Entitled 'Crime : Lock it and Stop it', this involved the painting of six of their ECW-bodied Bristol VRTs in a white livery with a red fluorescent band below their lower deck windows with the appropriate lettering, the scheme having been designed in the Group's own publicity studio, by now responsible for the design of all its publicity items, and sometimes gaining outside 'commissions' for publicity design work. Entering service in their new guise in April, these buses soon became a familiar sight in and around Hull where it was hoped that their message would be heeded.

More secondhand buses were obtained in April in the form of 3 ECW-bodied Bristol VRTs from Trent Motor Traction Co. Ltd. of Derby. Two of these were placed in service in the East Yorkshire fleet while the other joined Cherry Coaches. Also from Trent came a 1970 open-top ECW-bodied Bristol VRT to help Scarborough & District compete against the three operators by now running open-toppers on Scarborough's sea-front. On the debit side, Cherry Coaches withdrew its ex.Lincolnshire Road Car Co. ECW bus-bodied Bristol LH6L, a Plaxton-bodied Bedford SB5 coach and one of its two ex.Travelplan Freight Rover Sherpa minicoaches while Primrose Valley lost one of its Plaxton-bodied Ford R1114 coaches when this was burnt out. Bristol VRT 524 was modified to DiPTAC specification with a split level entrance and 544 & 546, two of the former London Country North East ECW-bodied Leyland Olympian coaches were re-registered from B108LPH & B110LPH to 344EYL & 546EYB respectively. By this time in fact, no less than 19 coaches had received 'cherished' registration numbers, almost all of which contained the letters 'EY', but including the Plaxton-bodied Leyland Tiger Cherrys 'flagship' which was 32CHY.

Continuing East Yorkshire's progressive vehicle replacement policy, 7 new 76-seat NCME-bodied, Gardner-engined Leyland Olympians arrived in May and were all

Originally numbered 191 in the East Yorkshire fleet, Plaxton-bodied Leyland Leopard OAT88V was transferred to the associated Cherry's Coaches company in 1988 and was subsequently renumbered 288. It is seen here in Cherry's livery carrying additional lettering in connection with the contract upon it was employed to Leos Food Superstore in Hull. (P.J.S.Shipp)

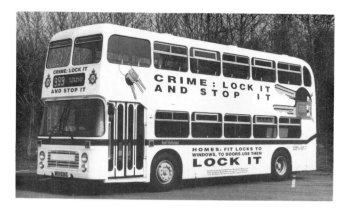

One of several East Yorkshire Bristol VRTs specially painted for an anti-crime campaign sponsored jointly by Hull South Crime Prevention Panel, East Yorkshire, Humberside Police and Hull Safer Cities in 1991 is 526 which was appropriately posed with its route number blinds set at '999'. (EYMS)

placed in service at the start of the following month. These replaced a number of older Atlanteans and were used mainly on services in the Hull area. A fifth National Expressliner with identical Volvo chassis and Plaxton Paramount body also arrived in September to replace an existing coach now too old for the National Express contract.

The Fylingdales contract at Scarborough had by now come up for renewal and having been again the successful bidder, the company needed some more modern coaches to replace the ten-year old Leyland Leopards acquired with the Wallace Arnold business in 1987. Accordingly, 4 Leyland Tigers with Duple coachwork and 1 Tiger with a Plaxton Paramount body dating from 1982/3 were acquired, three of them in the

yellow & blue livery of Kinch's of Leicestershire. To avoid confusion with service vehicles, this trio remained in these colours and the others two were painted to match, along with East Yorkshire Paramount-bodied Tiger fleet number 5 which was also allocated to Scarborough & District for the contract and one of the original Leopards which was retained as a spare.

It had been decided that neither the Leyland Lynx nor the Optare Delta, evaluated the previous year, would be suitable for the Scarborough - Helmsley route, being too expensive for a rural service and having front overhangs which were too long and too low for the country lanes and tight turns on this route, now being marketed to tourists as the 'Valerider'. It was therefore decided to consider rebodying up to six Leyland Leopards with bus-style bodies, utilising the best chassis from amongst the Fylingdales contract fleet and the similar vehicles with Plaxton Supreme bodies already operating the route from Pickering depot. Accordingly, Fylingdales Leopard 236 was despatched to East Lancashire Coachbuilders in August to be rebodied for trial purposes, returning home in its new form towards the end of December. It is intended that the remaining Leyland Leopards from Fylingdales (which incidentally remained until now in their Wallace Arnold colours, albeit without fleet names) and Pickering would either be sold or refurbished and cascaded to the Primrose Valley and Cherry Coaches fleets to replace older coaches. Perhaps more surprising is the decision to despatch six Leyland Nationals to East Lancashire Coachbuilders for rebuilding to Greenway specification. Five of the buses concerned are East Yorkshire's 179/80/5/6/7, short B-series Nationals which were withdrawn from service some three years ago and have since remained in store whilst the sixth - to be numbered 184 - is a dual-door example purchased in November 1991 from Lucketts garages (Watford) Ltd. On the new vehicle front, a further ten NCME-bodied Leyland Olympians with Gardner

Right : East Yorkshire NCME-bodied Leyland Olympian 555 is one of the company's newest double deckers. seven of which entered service in 1991. A further ten buses of this type are currently on order for delivery in 1992. (P.J.S.Shipp)

Below : One of the buses borrowed from its manufacturer for evaluation purposes during 1991 was Leyland Lynx demonstrator F74DCW which wore Cynon Valley's ivory, orange & green livery. (K.A.Jenkinson)

6LXB engines, ZF 4-speed automatic gearboxes and full DiPTAC features - to be numbered 561-70 - have been ordered for delivery in April 1992 while also on order is one of the first ten production versions of the new Optare Spectra double decker which is to be numbered 571 and used for evaluation purposes to help East Yorkshire decide on the best vehicle for its future double-deck replacement policy

In 1991 the Group's latest property acquisition was made, this being the house at 256 Anlaby Road, thus bringing into the company's ownership after 62 years all five of the row of houses, all that were left after the demolition of the western end of the row to make was for the Anlaby Road flyover in the '60s. Of interest to visitors to the Group's head office is the fact that the easternmost house, 252, next to the garage, still contains some of the stained glass windows presumably installed when the house was built for its original purpose -

*Scarborough & District's former Wallace Arnold/ Hardwicks Leyland Leopard 236 (PNW336W) was in December 1991 fitted with a new East Lancashire Coachbuilders body equipped with coach-type seating for use on the Scarborough - Pickering service for which a 'Valerider' logo was added immediately behind the rear wheel arch. (P.J.S.Shipp)*

*One of the short B-series Leyland Nationals currently being rebuilt by East Lancashire Coachbuilders to Greenway specification is 187 which is seen wearing all-over red livery in Princes Street, Bridlington on 5 July 1988 while working the 122 service to Scarborough. (K.A.Jenkinson)*

the vicarage for Holy Trinity Church in Hull Old Town. The present managing director's office is presumably the vicar's bedroom !

Also on the property front, the year has seen the building of a new canteen on East Yorkshire's land at the back of Hull coach station, following British Rail's wish to terminate the lease of the travel office in the station which is to be transferred into the previous canteen premises further west in the same side of the station. At Scarborough the company's bus station at Valley Bridge also closed, with the few remaining long distance route terminal points dispersed to town centre streets and travel and administrative offices to a three-storey house at 4 Alma Square, adjacent to main bus stops in Westborough. After the Wallace Arnold/Hardwicks acquisitions in 1987, the Group owned or leased no less than eight properties in Scarborough - the latest disposal reduced this to just three !

In contrast to the situation in the mid-'eighties when a fleet total down to little more than 150 vehicles gave rise to doubts that East Yorkshire could survive as a separate entity, 1991 sees the Group fleet at over 330 vehicles, which with the travel agencies and rail charter business produce an annual turnover of over £13million, the company in profit and with a healthy bank balance.

In the 71 years since East Yorkshire's foundations were laid and the first service was opened from Elloughton to Hull, the company has passed from private enterprise to become a member of a large group and then through state ownership back to the private sector, thus completing the full circle. During this time, its vehicles have become a familiar sight in and around North Humberside and North Yorkshire and as a result of the acquisition of a great many of its competitors,

the EYMS Group has grown both in stature and importance. The past five years have brought the Group into a new era - one of declining numbers wishing to avail themselves of public transport services, one of ever-rising costs and, as a consequence of the 1985 Transport Act, one of new and ever-increasing competition. Despite all these hurdles, the EYMS Group has, through its tireless efforts and forward thinking, continued to succeed and travel from strength to strength and with its present highly experienced management team and many supportive and long-serving employees. It will doubtless remain in a position of prominence within its area of operation throughout the current decade and beyond. Looking to the future, the EYMS Group has aspirations of diversification into other related fields whilst firmly maintaining its bus and coach operations as its core business and as such, will provide much for future writers who it is hoped will continue to chronicle the Group's history well into the next century.